THE GOD GAME

It's Your Move

THE GOD GAME

It's Your Move

Reclaim Your Spiritual Power

Leo Booth

STILLPOINT PUBLISHING

STILLPOINT PUBLISHING
Building a society that honors the Earth,
Humanity, and The Sacred in All Life.

For a free catalog or ordering information, write
Stillpoint Publishing, Box 640, Walpole, NH 03608, USA
or call
1-800-847-4014 TOLL-FREE (Continental US, except NH)
1-603-756-9281 (Foreign and NH)

This book is manufactured in the United States of America.
Cover and text designed by Karen Savary.

Published by Stillpoint Publishing, Box 640
Meetinghouse Road, Walpole, NH 03608

The God Game: It's Your Move

ISBN: 0-913299-99-5

Library of Congress Cataloging in Publication Data
94-67882

1 3 5 7 9 8 6 4 2

This book is printed on chlorine-free recycled paper
to save trees and preserve Earth's ecology.

Dedication

This book is dedicated to my marketing director,
Sharon McGinley, and my personal editor, Kate Russell,
not forgetting Thom, the office cat, who believes he is a dog and teaches
all of us tranquility and unconditional love.

CONTENTS

ACKNOWLEDGMENTS

I'VE ALWAYS FELT THAT WRITING A BOOK IS AN ADVENTURE, AN EXCITing *move* in translating personal ideas and feelings into print. In this sense, writing a book is playing the God Game, especially when the book is about re-claiming spiritual power that I believe is the *essential* gift that God has given to all of us. *Our* responsibility is to use that Gift. That's the basic move of the God Game.

Although you can play a game alone, it is more fun when we play with others. In the writing of this book there have been many players. I've already dedicated this book to the staff at my office, Spiritual Concepts. However, a special mention must be made of Kate Russell. Not only is she my personal editor, but she has the unique ability of understanding my thoughts and ideas—often before I do! Although Kate is not religious, the occasional times she has attended my lectures and Recovery Service, someone usually asks, "Is that woman a nun?" No, Kate is definitely not a nun, but she is theological, philosophical and spiritual. She has been a tremendous help both in the development and editing of this book. Her moves have been extremely inspiring.

The *staff and congregation* at St. George's Episcopal Church in Hawthorne, California, outside Los Angeles, also need mention because most of the ideas found in *The God Game* have been practiced and "worked on" within my congregation. Their patience and support have been nurturing.

The Bishops and members of the Diocese here in Los Angeles also need thanks and appreciation. Never have I experienced interference or censorship from my Church in any phase of my journey to reclaim spiritual empowerment. My criticisms and frustrations with the church have always been heard and nurtured supportively. God willing, I am helping the Episcopal Church as well as all religions become a safer place by writing this book.

Everyone at Stillpoint Publishing has been a joy to work with. They demonstrate a spiritual theme that runs throughout the book, that we need to be flexible, adaptable and inclusive—forever open to changes. The creative exchanges between our offices have usually resulted in a completely new idea or concept, namely because we were prepared to *hear*. Publishers Errol Sowers and Meredith Young-Sowers, and their editor, Ann Weil Richards, together with their staff, have often unknowingly enabled the spiritual moves of the God Game to run smoothly. I am truly grateful.

I don't believe spirituality grows totally in isolation. Therefore, my deep gratitude goes to all of the people who have written to me, or talked with Sharon and Kate, about their own pain and recovery, and to the many who attend my workshops and lectures and take time to speak with me after. You made the first moves that led to the God Game, and I honor your courage and wish you well in your recovery. The stories and anecdotes found in *The God Game* are composites drawn from the letters, conversations and experiences of people who I have met. Special thanks go to Ruth, Kathleen, Georgette, Larry, Gail, and others who gave permission to have part of their writings reproduced, and who have allowed me to blend their stories with others to retain anonymity. You touch and move me. We must all connect to something, and your connection with me has inspired this book.

I must also thank all those recovery support groups who, just by being there, enable me to feel secure enough to write yet another book on spiritual empowerment. The fact that I believe this book is *unique* and different comes from listening to and digesting the abundant ideas of recovery. *The God Game* is my next step to my healing—and I acknowledge my role in this move to personal empowerment.

INTRODUCTION

I WROTE MY FIRST BOOK ABOUT SPIRITUALITY OVER TEN YEARS AGO, and sometimes it seems that I've been talking about spirituality ever since. The original title of that book was *Walking On Water: Spirituality and Recovery*, and it begins like this:

> To walk on water is to experience the joy in living. Know the laugh and the human embrace as well as the tear. Walking on water is seeing and feeling the given miracle of life in every moment. It is the shouted "yes" to all that life will bring.[1]

In those days, I was truly "walking on water," vibrant with a joy and a new understanding of spirituality I had never imagined was possible. Barely seven years earlier, I had nearly been thrown out of the priesthood for my drinking. In treatment, it was suggested that I take a long hard look at the unhealthy way I had been using religion and my priesthood to gain a sense of power and self-worth. I didn't want to take that look. I didn't want to accept that some of my treatment mates were far more spiritual than I. I nearly quit treatment. I thought of leaving the priesthood. Anything but face myself.

But I stayed, determined to discover the healthier, happier relationship with God I saw in others. Freed from the numbing effects of alcohol and religiosity, I came alive. "Say Yes To Life!" became my theme, my mantra, my call to arms. I began to work with other addicts and alcoholics, and eventually moved from England to America to work in various treatment programs. I started my own consultancy business because I wanted to share this exciting "YES!" to life with others—the yes to ourselves and to God that recovery from addictions, depression, and low self-esteem can bring.

I began talking about the difference between spirituality and religion, trying to help people understand that they need not be religious to be spiritual. But I kept meeting so many people who desperately wanted to say YES, who struggled long and hard even with treatment, therapy, and support groups, and still wound up saying NO to themselves and to God. I dug deep into the issues, tugging and pulling at the various problems—the Adult Child issues, the abuse issues, the addictions and cross-addictions, trying to discover what was keeping so many people from saying YES to life. I realized that many were experiencing something I myself had gone through.

Stuck at the bottom of all that pain was a deeply embedded core of beliefs and behaviors that I identified as "Religious Addiction" or "Religious Abuse." In *When God Becomes a Drug: Breaking the Chains of Religious Addiction and Abuse*, I described the symptoms and sources of religious abuse. I thought this would help remove the barricades to help people overcome their guilt and shame and begin to develop a healthy spirituality.

But this confusing "Yes . . . but NO" reaction persisted. Hospitals and administrators liked the concept, but wouldn't—or couldn't—apply it. Patients themselves kept smacking up against this same bizarre block: "Yes, I want to change my relationship with God, but . . . it's not working."

Why? I kept asking myself. Why isn't it working? As I spoke with patients and people attending my conferences across the country, it seemed that people were trying to change themselves without really changing their view of God. This confusion arose because it often *looked* like they were changing their view of God. Some would change religions to move away from a rigid, shame-based doctrine to one that encouraged openness and tolerance; others "took a vacation" from religion altogether, thinking that might open the door to a healthier relationship with God. Often to no avail.

The answer to this perplexing problem came in a chance conversation. It was a transformative moment for me. A woman shared a remarkable story of having grown up in a traditional Southern Baptist family. In her late fifties, she divorced her abusive alcoholic husband, addressed her own alcoholism, and began working on her co-dependency and self-esteem issues. She railed against the religious system that had kept her submissive and subservient her whole life. "I'm finally growing up and learning how to have adult relationships," she said. "But nobody ever told me how to have a grown-up relationship with God!"

There was the answer! It had been dangling in front of me, tantalizingly close, but it took one woman's courageous outcry to bring it into focus. The problem was the childish, dependent relationship with God fostered by the majority of religious messages that have been ingrained into religions and even into the fabric of society for years. Here was the source of the co-dependency and powerlessness that seemed to resist the best therapy and years of recovery and support group work. For all the hard work, for all the changes made, somehow, people were not really changing their *Core Beliefs* about God. And no wonder: everything they were hearing from religion, and often even from therapy, reinforced a confusing, conflicted, disempowered relationship with God.

So began the next part of my own spiritual journey. It has led me to evolve a new model of spirituality based on building a relationship between body, mind, and emotions. And it has led me to challenge and confront my beliefs about God, religion, and spirituality that perpetuate this childish, disempowering relationship with God—*without rejecting religion.*

I have not left the church. I have not abandoned my basic belief in Christianity. I believe there are aspects of Christianity that I have outgrown, and which may need to be rejected or revised, and I think the same is true of other religions. I am convinced that a healthy use of religion can enhance spirituality, but I also believe that healthy spirituality is not dependent on—or absolutely linked to—religion, or even a belief in God.

With this new insight, I began to re-examine the questions that come to my office. The majority fall into two categories: "Why can't I change how I feel about God?" and "How do I create a healthy relationship with God?" *When God Becomes a Drug* provided partial answers to these questions by identifying religious addiction and abuse, and suggesting ways to move out of an abusive system.

Now it's time to move into the next phase: reclaiming the spiritual power lost to dysfunctional or outmoded religious messages. You can do this by learning to identify unhealthy religious messages to see how they have molded your beliefs about God, and then learn new tools for revising or moving away from them.

I call this process the God Game. Over the years, I've listened to people who say they feel like pawns God uses in some cosmic scheme. Feeling like a pawn keeps them stuck in a powerless, dependent, fear-based relationship with God. When I look at my feeling of "walking on water" I realize it comes from feeling like I'm a player in the Game of Life with God. Not a game in the win-lose meaning, or game in the sense of being the object of a hunt, but game in the sense of "having a spirit of adventure."

When I first began working on this book, my visual image of the God Game alternated between a chess game, with its many moves and rules, and a sort of "Trivial Pursuit," with paths leading out of a box in the center to a circle on the outside. The box in the middle is the *God-Box*—that collection of Core Beliefs and religious messages accumulated over the years that limit our spiritual power and keep us stuck in a childish, dependent relationship with God rather than a mature partnership.

Although I dropped the image of the board game, the God-Box remains, as well as the idea that in order to move from being a spiritual pawn to powerful player with God, we must acknowledge our God-Box, examine the beliefs and attitudes inside it and be willing to let go of them, or learn to transform them from disempowering messages to empowering beliefs.

When I first brought my spirituality program into hospitals, treatment programs and counseling centers, I kept running up against a concept called "Body-Mind-Spirit." I'd talk about spirituality as being the relationship between Body, Mind and Emotions, and the Marketing Departments of these facilities would proudly send me literature proclaiming that Father Leo was serving as a consultant to help patients heal in Body-Mind-*Spirit*. "NO! NO! NO!" I'd insist. "*Spirit*—spirituality—*must* include all three aspects of being human: Mental, Emotional, and Physical!"

But the Body-Mind-Spirit concept has been around so long, and is so ingrained in religious and philosophical thought, that sometimes I feel like I'm banging my head against a brick wall trying to get people to understand the difference. The Body-Mind-Spirit concept actually contributes to the spiritual breakdown we experience because it reinforces the belief that spirituality is *outside* of us, on a separate plane or a higher level of being. This is one of the major stumbling blocks to creating whole, healthy spirituality. People have been trying to heal the whole person using a spiritual model that puts spirituality in a separate place, and leaves our emotions out altogether. No wonder people keep thinking they have to "get" spiritual, and can't quite grasp the idea that we are *born* spiritual—that our spirituality is built in. We *are* spiritual beings, but at some point in our lives, usually in childhood, we are taught to look *outside ourselves* for spirituality, to "transcend" our humanness in order to become more spiritually elevated. This sent us off on a spiritual wild goose chase, for spirituality is already inside us.

The God Game is about discovering the spirituality within every one of us and, in the process, finding God. Our moves in the God Game bring us into a powerful, adult relationship with God that is a partnership, a co-creatorship, rather than passive dependency. Playing the God Game involves moving away from some long-held beliefs about the relationship between spirituality, God, and religion. It's a process of transforming beliefs or behaviors that harm us instead of trying to transcend them. The God Game is an exciting adventure— and a difficult and scary process to confront some of the pain in our lives. But once you learn how to make the moves—make the choices and take actions—you, too, may find that in good times or bad, you are still enjoying being a powerful player with God. Then, I hope, you will truly begin to shout "YES!" to life.

NOTES

1. "To walk on water . . . " Booth, Father Leo. *Spirituality and Recovery: A Guide to Positive Living.* (Deerfield Beach, FL: Health Communications, 1985). p. 1.

THE
GOD
GAME

It's Your Move

1

A New Understanding of Spirituality

> I've tried different religions, and that didn't help.
> Then I decided maybe religion was getting in the
> way, so I tried Yoga and other forms of meditation.
> I've been in all kinds of spirituality study groups, and
> learned lots of new things. But I still don't feel close
> to God, and I don't understand. Why can't I seem to
> get spiritual?
>
> *Sandra*

"WHY CAN'T I SEEM TO GET SPIRITUAL?" THIS IS THE QUESTION I'M
asked most often and with such a range of feelings: bewilderment, confusion, anger, frustration, shame, and sadness. Alongside these feelings,
a sense of lostness, loneliness and yearning fairly leaps out of the eyes,
off the pages of letters, out of the voices on the telephone. I know that
confusion, that loneliness, that yearning. I know it intimately because I
have had to move through it many times. In order to make those moves
I had to open myself to a whole new understanding of what spirituality is and how it works in the world. It was a difficult process, and it's
still ongoing, but the result has been a deeper spiritual awareness than
I ever thought possible, and a mature co-creatorship with God that
enriches and empowers all aspects of my life.

I grew up believing that religion was the only way to reach God, and that when you reached God, you were spiritual. Of course, at that time I didn't put it in those terms. As a little boy in England, religion and God were chained to the violent religious arguments between my parents. My father is a Roman Catholic of Irish descent and my mother is Anglican (Episcopal). If I thought about spirituality at all, it was probably in terms of peace and quiet and escape from the religious prejudices that were tearing apart our home and, in many ways, my country. Unhealthy religious attitudes were causing most of my problems, and yet I was raised to believe that it was only *through religion* that I could be spiritually happy.

I used religion and the priesthood as a means to escape the pain and conflicts of my childhood. Becoming a priest was undoubtedly my way to put an end to the fighting that plagued my home life, for no matter how divided they may have been, both my parents regarded the clergy as the higher authority on matters pertaining to God and religion. Of course, I hadn't a clue then that these Core Beliefs were driving me. I knew I felt "called" to the priesthood, but I thought it was God "up there" calling me, not the confused, fearful little boy inside me who cried himself to sleep beneath the covers while my parents raged at each other in the name of God.

All during my youth, up to and even throughout my treatment for alcoholism, I was motivated by the belief that religion was the only path to God. I really didn't know what it was supposed to feel like when I finally reached God. I know there was a "high" that I got from the drama, the pageantry and ritual of the Church, and I always connected this feeling of exhilaration with God. Other than that, I don't know what I expected my life to be like. I may have thought I wouldn't feel badly about myself any more, wouldn't be lonely or feel embarrassed about my nervous stuttering or hurt when I fell in and out of love, wouldn't be tempted by any of those "seven deadly sins" and other religious taboos. I thought the way to God was to transcend all my earthly pleasures and delights. And since I quite liked many of those pleasures, I was in great grief and conflict over the idea that I *shouldn't* like them and would have to give them up if I wanted God's blessing.

In my youth, I probably confused spirituality with "being holy"— trying to follow the examples of the saints, going on retreats to monasteries, wearing ritual clothes for the Mass, and swinging incense, praying for long periods on my knees, or fasting. And even though there was a lot of "busyness" in all these activities, most of them required a lot of passivity, an emphasis on disconnecting from the world in order to "be still" and know God. So I grew up with a very limited idea of how and where to find God, and what kinds of feelings were "Godly" or "spiritual."

SOME COMMON BELIEFS ABOUT SPIRITUALITY

Perhaps you share the same experience of being taught that spirituality is "out there" somewhere, that we "get" spiritual through the use of religious ceremonies, rituals or exercises, or by following certain rules or precepts. If you have been using the "Body-Mind-Spirit" concept to understand your spirituality, you might not recognize how this model adds to the belief that spirituality is separate—in a different realm— from body and mind. Many people have shared with me a common belief that prayers, meditations, and exercises such as yoga or Zen are the tools we use to somehow *overcome* or *transcend* our human imperfections so that we can unite body and mind with spirit.

This was certainly my experience with religion—the Mass, the liturgy, the rituals, scriptures, prayers and doctrines were all focused on bringing the Holy Spirit into my life, and helping me overcome my "base" human nature. As I said earlier, I actively sought that "high," believing that it was the way I'd know I was connecting to God. I've seen many people get that same dreamy "not here" look when discussing metaphysics, the Bible, the Alcoholics Anonymous "Big Book," Zen, or Eastern mysticism. No matter what our religious background, it seems we have all been ingrained with the idea that spirituality is some place *other* than where we are—some exalted level beyond real humanness.

This was the path I followed until I went to treatment for my alcoholism. I often tell the story of old Harry who, by just being himself, provided a vital transforming moment in my life—one perhaps even more transforming than the car crash that put me into treatment. After only a few days in treatment, I'd had enough. Nobody was giving me the "respect" I thought I deserved. I packed my bags and was on my way out when old Harry confronted me. "Leo, you're full of shit. But you can get better," he said. "You've got to get square with the God inside you—then you can really start getting well." My addict's ego and stubbornness sent me upstairs to unpack; I decided to finish treatment, determined to prove the old guy wrong.

I didn't know it then, but Harry had just become my role model for how to be spiritual. I wasn't sure what he had, or why I didn't have it, but I knew, in the moments following that brief encounter, that I wanted more than anything to discover that God with whom I could be comfortable. It was the shock of my life to realize that this penniless, unsophisticated old drunk had a deeper spirituality and connection to God than all my education and training had given me. Although it would be many years before I could define it or talk about it, in those first days of recovery, I began to understand that spirituality is not "gotten" by way of religion and ritual and rules. It has been, and always will be, within us without end: the creative spark that connects us to each other, and with God.

It took a lot of hard work to begin to discover that creative spark within me, and to learn how to use it. Sometimes I laugh when people in Twelve Step programs assume that because I am a clergyman, I had no problem with the "spiritual part" of the program. Fortunately, my therapists knew that precisely because I was a priest, I'd have a hard time stepping down off my religious know-it-all pedestal and finding healthy spirituality. I had spent my life praying in church, meditating at holy shrines throughout England, saying the rosary and wearing blessed medallions and yet I still ended up an alcoholic. "What's the use of prayer?" I asked. "How can I make God hear me?" They said, "Pray for willingness to open your mind to something new." One of the hardest moves I had to make in my recovery was to shift my thinking a bit—not a radical 180 degree turn, but just a little shift, a small opening of the door to a different way of thinking. I didn't have to fling open the door and jump out, blinking in the blinding glare of sudden spiritual transformation. I only had to crack open the door a little bit and peep out, just to see what might be there. No, my moves were not dramatic overnight conversions, but a slow process of moving into a new understanding of spirituality.

My first moves were simply about connecting God with nature, poetry, dance, and through expressing my feelings. And I also began to find God in the pain, in shame, even in the "Bogeyman" God who often terrorized my childhood dreams.

But something was still missing. ME. I was missing myself, my connection, my part in the relationship with God. It was wonderful to be finding God in so many new places, but what was I supposed to be doing with God? What did finding God in the odd places of life mean to me? What was I finding when I discovered God in all those different places? The answer eventually became clear: I was finding *me*. I was finding within myself the spiritual power and peace I'd been seeking outside myself all my life. I came to understand that when I laughed and cried with Charlie Chaplin, I was connecting with God through my responses—through my identification of my own feelings. No wonder my life had felt so empty despite all the religious activity I'd packed into it. Having been told God was to be found through only one path, I had missed or discounted all the other places I'd been connecting with God and hadn't realized it.

This was the embryonic beginning of the idea of the God Game. The sense of adventure that required my moves if I were ever to get really comfortable with not only *who* I am, but *what* I am. This was the beginning of my new spiritual relationship with God, not as a pawn, but as a vital player.

I realized then that the secular world is rich with many ways, great and small, to connect with God. I came to understand how having been denied the opportunities to learn how to develop and grow from the connections to God I was finding outside religion left me feeling spiritually incomplete. I had been taught to look up and away from myself for spiritual power, and to search inside myself for the "bad" things I wanted God to change or take away. I began to see how this damaged my relationship with myself, with other people, and with God. This "one way only" approach was limiting my understanding of spirituality to the religiously sacred and was not showing me how to recognize and use my own spiritual power.

As I started working with a new concept of spirituality, I began to hear things differently, and respond to them differently. All my life I'd heard "the Kingdom of God is within you" but I hadn't really thought about what that meant, except from the religious standpoint—the Christian concept of God's grace having been bestowed on us. Now I began to look at it from a different perspective. I began to talk about the "God within," and learning to be positive and creative. I started seeing spiritual power in the choices I made, in the steps I took to make changes in my life. At last, I started to understand what it was that Harry had that *I* wanted: *spiritual empowerment.*

My process, my spiritual journey, has been a series of small moves like this one. It is a journey away from a set of beliefs that boxed God into one place—which for me was religion—and into a new understanding of spirituality that creates for me an exciting new connection and relationship with God.

Spirituality: The Gift Within

Each of us contains a spark of divinity, and that spark enables us to connect with each other and with God. None of us is more or less "divine" than another, regardless of culture or faith. And the path to spiritual completion is in the moves we make to come together, within ourselves individually, and with our world as a whole.

I have come to believe that spirituality is the "soul" of religion, rather than religion being the path to spirituality. This spiritual soul unites nearly all religions, regardless of dogma or faith, for all religions seek to reflect the essential virtues and qualities that bind the relationship between God and human beings.

I did not come to this understanding of spirituality overnight. When I really started listening to myself saying "The Kingdom of God is within you," or "Spirituality is becoming a positive and creative human being," I had to sit down and think about what that really meant. *What is* the Kingdom of God? Did we always have it? Are we born with it? If we aren't born with it, at what point in our lives is it bestowed on us? Is it a Christian kingdom or does the Kingdom of God within us transcend religion? What would God's kingdom within me look like? What do we humans possess that reflects the Kingdom of God?

Human beings have a tremendous capacity for good, I decided. Then the theologian in me immediately countered with, "Yeah, but what about our capacity for evil—where does that fit in the Kingdom of God?" I had many such dialogues with myself, and still do, as I widen my understanding of human spirituality. I thought back over all the things that had moved me in theology and philosophy, and began to list some important qualities I felt were universal. I began talking about the Spiritual Values of Love, Forgiveness, Courage, Truth, Honesty, and the like. Eventually, these evolved into four main Spiritual Values or qualities: Truth, Love, Change, and Harmony. They are linked to each other and the thread they make is woven into the fabric of my spirituality. These have become the cornerstones of the Kingdom of God within me. They have become vital to my moves in the God Game. And they can serve you as well.

TRUTH

What is Truth? In my university days, I would spend long hours drinking with my friends, discussing and debating many exalted notions of what Truth was and where it was found. I saw Truth as something Cosmic, "out there," bigger than me, something to be sought, aspired to. Even without a drop of alcohol, I'd get drunk on heady discussions of the "Truth" in Oscar Wilde, or in Tennyson, or even in Mozart and Picasso. For all that I found Truth in those places, I didn't understand how it worked in my life, except as an "Exalted Precept" by which to live.

Among my boyhood heroes were Saint Augustine and Charlie Chaplin. Both of them touched me in different ways. I admired Augustine's ideas and writings, especially when he said, "We are restless 'til we rest in God." I understood that restlessness, that yearning. Yet Charlie Chaplin's Little Tramp touched me too with his gentle acceptance of his own humanness. To me, Chaplin personified that restlessness—my restlessness. The "Truth" that I found in both Chaplin and Saint Augustine was truth about me—the reality of my own loneliness and yearning for acceptance.

The Spiritual Value of Truth involves seeing things as they really are, avoiding denial, manipulation, and dishonest behavior that stops us seeing or facing reality. It is the honest acceptance of who we are, and how we are in the world. Some call it integrity or honesty. I've heard people say, "I must stand in my own truth" when they are fighting not to give up something important to themselves. The Spiritual Value of Truth allows us to recognize and express what we feel and think, rather than masking our real selves in order to gain acceptance.

Living in Truth allows us to "be real." The Truth about Leo is that he is an ordinary man who often seeks to do extraordinary things. For a long time I believed that to achieve the extraordinary, I had to *be* extraordinary. I thought that meant I had to be brilliant in all areas, perfect, and right. The truth was, trying to be extraordinary only made me arrogant, egotistical, and very, very lonely. What I discovered is that the more I allow myself to just be Leo, an ordinary person, the more I find myself doing things I never thought possible.

For example, I absolutely loathe having to deal with any kind of legal paperwork—bank loans, contracts, and the like. Yet they are a necessary part of my work as both a priest and addictions consultant. So despite the fact that I'd much rather have somebody else do these things for me, I found myself on the phone one day, gritting my teeth and demanding that the loan officer explain in everyday English what a certain clause meant. In the process, I learned more of the Truth about myself: even though I hate doing some things, *I can* do them. In the old days, I would have confused not liking something with not being able to do it, and I wouldn't have even tried, thus setting myself up either to be totally dependent on an accountant or having my loan denied because I hadn't understood some of the terms. For many people this might be a very ordinary, mundane experience. For me, it was quite extraordinary.

This is how Truth empowers me. First, I was honest with myself, then, I was honest with the bank official—"I don't understand what that means. Please explain it." Truth lets me admit mistakes. I think this is true humility—not the sort of false piety that some people associate with being humble, but simply having a good grasp on my own reality. Truth lets me acknowledge my strengths as well as my weaknesses. From this truth springs my creativity.

When I talk about being creative, I don't mean exclusively in the artistic sense that people associate with music, art, or writing. I define human creativity as the ability to respond mentally, emotionally, and physically to our world. Our creativity comes with the ability to feel, to reason, to evaluate, then make choices and take action. Our ability to respond determines how we create solutions to problems, how we create relationships. When we are fully connected within ourselves, we are in touch with—and aware of—how our bodies, minds, and emotions work together. The more clearly our bodies, minds, and emotions communicate with each other, the more completely we are able to respond, and thus, our creative potential increases.

For instance, when I began to talk to the bank official, I noticed my heart was pounding, my nervous stutter returned, and I heard myself being alternately snappish or flippant—always a signal for me that I am too agitated. Recognizing these signals, I took some slow, deep breaths while the bank official went over the form. "Careful, Leo," I told myself. "You don't want to blow this!" It was at this point that I told the man I was a bit confused about what he was asking, and requested that he explain it in a different manner.

Suppose I did not connect my irritability and stuttering with my confusion about what the man was telling me? What if I hadn't recognized that my heart was pounding or that I was becoming angry? I would probably have ticked the man off and my financial problem would have gotten worse instead of being resolved.

When we cease being real and honest with ourselves and each other, our Spiritual Truth becomes distorted; we diminish our connectedness and, in the process, erode our spiritual power. Revealing our own Truth does not always guarantee that others will respond in Truth, although they generally do. In my case, I exposed my ignorance to the banker; I risked ridicule, or worse, being taken advantage of. And taking risks is a crucial element in the God Game.

One of the hardest truths to accept is that we do not live in a perfect world. Our world contains joy and pain, light and dark. Accepting this Truth allows us to cope creatively with this duality within our natures. When we understand that to be human means to be imperfect, we can begin to embrace our imperfection. A friend shared with me this passage about the duality of our natures from a book of Cherokee teachings:

> It is all a process of change, of transformation, of refining transparency. There is no light without darkness. Many feel that darkness denotes something negative, but in the nighttime, the stars twinkle and in the nighttime the dreams grow, and those dreams determine our tomorrow. So nighttime, daytime, they are parts of the dream. One is neither bad nor good. It is how we approach those times that determines their value in our own life. So let us not fear the dark.[1]

This is a beautiful description of the spiritual power that accompanies acceptance of the imperfection and duality within our human nature and our world. Many of our most powerful moves will grow out of accepting this essential Truth.

LOVE

Truth opens the door to Love, probably the most widely explored and accepted spiritual quality. There are so many kinds of love: parent-child, brotherly and sisterly, love between friends, romantic love, sexual love, platonic love, self-love, and the so-called "agape" or universal love. No matter how it appears in our lives, love bridges our emotions, evoking a multitude of responses. How does it bridge the emotions? By the honest sharing of feelings, or expressions of our thoughts, not to mention the physical demonstrations of affection found in a friendly touch or hug, as well as sexual lovemaking. In sharing ourselves these ways, we allow ourselves to be understood. Perhaps more than any other quality, love has the capacity to still our restlessness or fill the "hole in our soul." Its presence in our lives can enrich and nourish us. Without it, we are spiritually malnourished and impoverished; we can wither and die.

What is it about Love that makes it such a widely cherished quality? The experience of Love tells us that we are not alone. Loving or being loved creates relationship. It does this by affirming what we feel and what we think about ourselves, God and other people. It is really difficult to love somebody we do not know. Obviously, we cannot know everything about a person. However, when we are able to hear or experience another person's deepest hopes, dreams or fears, and begin to share our own, then relationship is created. The honesty, integrity, and health of that relationship is determined by the degree to which we are able to reveal ourselves honestly to the other, and the honest responses that we receive.

That's why Truth, being honest about who we are, is so important, because if we present an illusion, or withhold some aspect of ourselves, we distort Love. Love can be as painful and agonizing as it is glorious and uplifting.

An important spiritual aspect of Love is forgiveness: accepting our humanness, forgiving our mistakes and those of others. Many people think that forgiveness is a spiritual "must." I have revised my thinking on that. We have the freedom to make choices, and sometimes, those choices are consciously designed to cause harm. I think there is a difference between making a mistake that hurts someone, or ourselves, and deliberately choosing to cause pain. Although forgiveness is an important spiritual aspect of Love, forgiving someone who abused you is not necessarily a prerequisite for healthy spirituality. Nor do I think that forgiveness means absolution from responsibility. There have been people who have hurt me, and whom I have forgiven, but I still hold them accountable for their behavior.

Forgiveness frees *me* first and foremost, and in most cases, it also frees the other person. When I forgive, I am able to move forward. I can continue or renew a relationship free of the pain, hurt, and misunderstandings. Even if the other person is no longer in my life, forgiveness frees me from resentment, from holding that person hostage in my bitterness. Perhaps your relationships suffer because you project past experiences with other people—a parent, a lover, a friend—onto someone else. You may end up punishing the innocent because you have not forgiven the actions of another. Without forgiveness, you can be held hostage to anger, hate, or victimization. Forgiveness can free you to see the people in your life for who they really are.

CHANGE

Change is the active ingredient in the transformative properties of spirituality. Our spiritual freedom revolves on Change. Without Change, I would have had nowhere to go when I confronted the truth, the reality of Leo. Yes, I was full of denial and self-deceit, *but I could change.* Despair and helplessness are born of the belief that we cannot change or get out of a situation. Without the freeing spiritual qualities of Change, we are indeed victims of whatever life hands to us—imprisoned, unable to move.

Yes, Change often involves pain. It was painful to confront some of the truths about myself. Yet that pain, coupled with the knowledge that I could change, forced me to take action. When you combine Truth and Change, you can access the transforming energy of spirituality.

A friend shared with me an analogy that helps her get through hard times: "When things just seem endlessly unbearable, I try to imagine an oyster having to live with an annoying piece of sand. I imagine the oyster trying all kinds of things to make that piece of sand go away before it goes to work and starts turning the sand into a pearl." I hadn't thought of it before, but that's a good analogy for how spirituality works within us. We use the resources with which we were created to transform a difficult situation. When we use those resources, we are using God's energy within us. We are co-creating with God.

Alongside Change comes the spiritual tool of *choice.* Because we can think, reason, and evaluate, we can make choices and take action. This is how we activate spirituality in our lives. It is in our choices that our partnership with God comes alive, for choice involves dialogue— not just inner dialogue with ourselves, but with others around us. It involves awareness of our feelings, and of our physical responses to what is going on.

Most of your moves in the God Game, in your partnership with God, are directed by your choices, the process you use to make them, and the way in which you evaluate and deal with the results of your choices.

Much of what I consider to be unhealthy spirituality comes from the belief that God or the Universe is *in control of us,* and we have very little choice in the matter. Some people seem to think of God as some kind of Cosmic Bus Driver who's got our route all mapped out for us. The only choice we get to make is whether to get on the Bus and let God drive without a lot of backseat driving on our part. This kind of thinking leads to spiritual powerlessness, for nobody likes relinquishing complete control that way. Have you ever taken a trip with someone who won't share the driving, doesn't look at a map, doesn't want you to make any kind of comment or suggestion about what roads to take, and usually has to be begged to stop for a restroom break? It's a pretty helpless, frustrating feeling, isn't it?

I have a friend who uses the analogy of God as Navigator: "I'm driving, but God's in the passenger seat beside me with all the maps. Now, I can choose to just jump on the freeway, and not even look at the map to see where I'm going, and then if I get lost, I'm frantically hollering at God to look at the map and find us a way out. Or, I can sit down with God before I make a move and figure out what routes to take. If there's some kind of traffic jam or road block, maybe I'll ask God to find an alternative route. It's my choice, my decision, about which route to take, or if I'm even going to bother to consult God at all." This is a good description of how co-creating with God can work. Instead of just going along with God for the ride, you take God along for the ride, and you can use God to help figure out which way to go, or not. It also works as a metaphor for dealing with choices that don't always take you where you want to go. Perhaps you didn't have the right information, or something beyond your control happens.

I think the most powerful aspect of spiritual choice is that we are rarely totally locked into a situation. There are always alternatives, even if it is to choose to change how we think about the situation.

Of course there are times when you get only one opportunity, and you've got to make the best decisions you can at the time. Later, you may see that perhaps a different approach would have made a difference. But for whatever reason—lack of information, not having strong enough choice-making skills—perhaps others are involved, you couldn't have done it differently. But you didn't know those things at the time, so don't beat yourself up over it—those choices weren't necessarily "bad." True, they did not create the results you may have wanted. However, you can learn from them so that if another similar opportunity arises, you can try something different. This is the real value of the freedom to choose, for it means we are not always doomed to making the same mistakes. It's still no guarantee that your choices will always work out for the best, but in feeling free to make these choices, you maintain your spiritual power.

Keep in mind that power and choice go hand in hand.

HARMONY

When something is in harmony, it is blended, balanced, attuned. Our freedom to choose, to change, opens the door to the Spiritual Value of Harmony. You can choose how to be, how to respond, what to do; you can make changes, shift your course to feel in alignment, in balance, to create Harmony in your life.

So many people describe peace or serenity as the absence of pain or conflict, and so are forever devastated when they can't "get to a place" where there isn't any pain, where there aren't any problems. Harmony does not imply an absence of pain and unpleasantness. In music, there are many jarring, discordant pieces that nevertheless reflect and employ all the technical properties of harmony. Harmony involves an order, a structure, even when the chords do not sound "pretty." Thus it is in life. To understand the spiritual value of Harmony is to live in balance with all that is within you and outside of you, to embrace the pain, face the problems, resolve the conflict. The Spiritual Value of Truth helps us face reality; Love to accept it, and possibly to forgive ourselves or others. We use Change to transform and move us into Harmony.

Like Love, Harmony brings the healing balm of acceptance, particularly self-acceptance. Harmony lets you accept your human limitations so that you can focus your energies on transforming them, like the oyster that quits trying to spit out the sand and instead accepts it and creates a pearl. Harmony brings all your spiritual powers into play— Truth, Love, and Change—to create Harmony.

These are the universal values that are reflected in much of the world's wisdom, religion, and philosophy. When I look at things that have excited me, ignited that "rush" I connected to God and spirituality, I find that whether it was the writings of T. E. Lawrence or Oscar Wilde or Teilhard de Chardin, or a movie like *Arthur*, or a Mass, or a quiet walk through my neighborhood, I am responding to one or more of these values. In that response, I find God.

The "You" In Spiritual:
The Spirituality of Being Real

Say the word *spiritual* out loud. Notice there's a "you" in spiritual. In fact, spirituality can be described as the "spirit of *you*." I used to think spirituality was about finding God. Now I understand that spirituality is about finding *me*, for when I discover me, I discover God at work within me. This is how I now understand the concept of "God Within" or the Kingdom of God within me. The Spiritual Values are part of me, are part of each of us. We just need to know where to look for them.

I have been writing for years about how we "miss ourselves" in so many aspects of our lives. As I began working with people who suffered from a broader variety of problems than just alcoholism, it troubled me that such a great majority had great difficulty acknowledging their own part in the miracles they were creating in their own lives. I've heard recovering alcoholics with years of sobriety saying "God got me sober," seemingly in total denial of their part—the daily choice not to drink, the meetings, phone calls, willingness to work on issues. In psychiatric treatment centers, I met people who were filled with despair, feeling they had no choices in life, unable to recognize what an incredibly powerful choice it was to enter treatment. I have had letters from people who share with me how they have worked through hard issues relating to childhood abuse, recovered from deep depression or addictions, but who don't "feel spiritual."

We miss ourselves when we are afraid to share our feelings. We miss ourselves when we discount our ideas, tell ourselves we're not good enough to do something. We miss ourselves when we ignore our health, don't exercise, don't feel good about our bodies. We miss ourselves when we seek to be perfect, and try to control everyone and everything around us. To deny our humanness is to miss ourselves. And when we miss ourselves, we miss God.

When I was a boy, I had a nervous stutter. I was very ashamed about it. Needless to say, I endured a great deal of teasing at school, which only caused me to further isolate myself from my peers. I discovered that when I felt very confident, my stutter disappeared. I joined the debating club to learn how to put a point across most effectively. I avoided discussions unless I felt well-versed in the subject so that I could be right, because if I was right, I wouldn't stutter. I hid my fear behind a facade of arrogance and superiority, and was always careful not to show emotions, lest I begin to stutter. In time, of course, disconnecting from myself in this way led to my alcoholism and my encounter with Harry. He saw through my facade—saw the scared, lonely little boy who stuttered. When Harry said to the grown Leo: "You're full of shit. But you can change," that was an invitation to *get real.*

Much of my journey since then has been about discovering the richness of being real and accepting that I am not perfect. I have my own foibles—my own weaknesses—many of them shaped by the circumstances of my childhood. I am learning that I am far more acceptable to other people, and to God, when I allow myself to be real.

One of my favorite stories is *The Velveteen Rabbit.* It contains many wonderful spiritual insights. One of the best is in the passage where the Skin Horse tells the Velveteen Rabbit about the process of becoming REAL:

> "What is REAL?" asked the rabbit one day . . . "Does it mean having things that buzz inside you and a stickout handle?"
>
> "Real isn't how you are made," said the skin horse. "It's a thing that happens to you. When a child loves you for a long, long time, not just to play with, but really loves you, then you become REAL."
>
> "Does it hurt?" asked the rabbit.
>
> "Sometimes," said the skin horse, for he was always truthful. "When you are real, you don't mind being hurt."
>
> "Does it happen all at once, like being wound up?" he asked, "or bit by bit?"
>
> "It doesn't happen all at once," said the skin horse. "You BECOME. It takes a long time. That's why it doesn't happen to people who break easily or have sharp edges, or who have to be carefully kept. Generally by the time you are REAL, most of your hair has been loved off, and your eyes drop out, and you get loose in the joints and very shabby. But these things don't matter at all, because once you are REAL, you can't be ugly, except to people who don't understand."[2]

When we are *real,* we discover our spiritual power. Being spiritually empowered is simply allowing ourselves to be human, possessing those qualities which make us uniquely ourselves as individuals, as well as the qualities we share as human beings.

Give yourself permission to think, look at things from different angles, make decisions and act on them. Certainly, you will have fears or reservations, and there are always areas in which you are not as skilled as you'd like to be, but don't let those stand in the way.

Becoming Real:
Connecting Body, Mind and Emotions

I have discovered that the more I try to hide the *real* Leo, the more empty I feel. Many people write or talk to me about this sense of feeling spiritually empty and disconnected, even when they are active in church or support groups. "What am I doing wrong?" is a question I hear far too often, and it saddens me. There's not a lot of "right" or "wrong" to spirituality. We are all spiritual beings. It's what we do with that spirituality that makes the difference.

As I've already mentioned, I view healthy spirituality as a process of connecting to ourselves, to that God within who is expressed in the Spiritual Values. Unhealthy spirituality is anything that disconnects us from ourselves and thus from God and our spiritual power.

Examining the causes of this sense of emptiness, I noticed that many religions and philosophies use something similar to the "Body-Mind-Spirit" concept I discussed earlier. It is supposed to show how the spirit is part of us. Yet, when I examine it, I find that it actually serves to divide the self, because it separates the spirit from the body and mind. This is one of those long-standing beliefs that must be confronted and revised because, for not only does this "triangle" divide and disconnect our spirituality, it reinforces the idea of being empty.

Most times, this triangle (with body, mind, and spirit at the three points) is drawn with nothing inside. If nothing is inside, then God's power must be outside, and we must *wait* for God to breathe into us so we will know what to do. Because this traditional view of spirituality teaches us to look outward for guidance, it feeds religious co-dependency and the need to be fixed, rescued or helped. It requires no interaction between the interconnected parts of ourselves, or with God, except that we merely continue to ask, plead, or pray, to be filled, guided, or used.

Like many spiritual concepts, I think that at one time, the "Body-Mind-Spirit" model was a good means to help people understand our connection to God. The religious teachers and philosophers of two thousand years ago had to use imagery people could readily understand. Can you imagine Moses trying to explain about the bacteria in undercooked pork to people who did not have microscopes or any clue as to the millions of living organisms invisible to the naked eye? They'd have laughed themselves silly or stoned him to death for being crazy.

But I don't think the Body-Mind-Spirit triangle works for us today. Only recently have we begun to understand how our emotions are interconnected to our minds and bodies. We have a great deal of information about the ways in which all three affect and react to each other.

Spirituality flows through *all* aspects of our being, through the unity of our bodies, minds and *emotions*. But the Body-Mind-Spirit triangle separates the spirit from the body and mind and leaves the emotions out entirely. The flowing spiritual energy is splintered, diminished, and spirituality ends up boxed inside a compartment all its own. This creates the idea of spirituality being in a different place, separate from vital aspects of humanness. So it's not surprising that people who

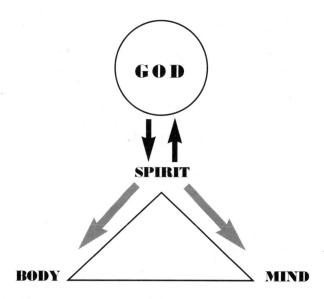

In the traditional diagram, God is seen as outside of us, with Spirit being separate from Mind and Body.

use "Body-Mind-Spirit" as their spiritual model feel empty, incomplete, and frustrated that they can't "get" spiritual.

Spiritual wholeness comes with the unity of physical, mental, and emotional qualities—our feelings, thoughts, actions. Healthy spirituality is the ability to discover and use those qualities. When we cannot see them, do not feel we have a right to use them, or feel we must discard or sublimate some part of ourselves, we are spiritually wounded. I prefer a spiritual model that shows how all three aspects of ourselves are linked: mental, emotional, and physical, and places God's power within us.

In my model, God is the source of the spiritual energy that radiates from our core. It is not something outside of us that we must try to capture or entice into us. It is already there, reflected in the unity of our mental, emotional, and physical responses. God is transcendent; God's power flows through the universe. But God's power is also immanent, within us; we access God's power with the healthy relationship between our body, mind and emotions. Also, the mental, emotional and physical aspects are linked; they affect each other.

How we feel about ourselves, and how we treat ourselves, is often

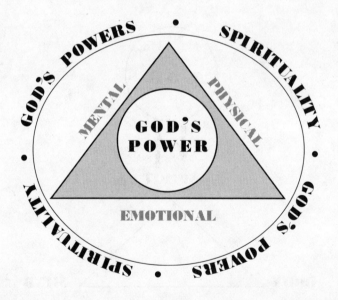

My diagram illustrates how God's Power within us radiates through us and ignites our spiritual energy through the union of Body, Mind, and Emotions.

a measure of our spiritual health. When I say that healthy spirituality requires mental, emotional, and physical well-being, I don't mean we must be *perfectly* healthy to be spiritually well. I have met many people who have incredible spirituality despite physical illnesses or limitations, or who suffer from an organic psychological disorder like manic depression. Their self-acceptance and self-esteem allow them to live positively and creatively with their problems.

I began to evolve this model of body-mind-emotions after telling my congregation "we need to pray less and exercise more," in a sermon. I'd noticed that many of my church members, including myself, were praying for various activities we needed to develop at the church, but the energy and activity tended to stop with the prayers. For me, the challenge of a spiritual approach leads to action. After the service, I really started thinking about all the implications of what I had said. I was paraphrasing one of my favorite sayings from Martin Luther King "We should pray, but we should also be prepared to march." I had been using that quote for a long time without really examining all that it meant. I had begun to see that the march—the physical move—was as much a prayer as the traditional form of prayer. That added new meaning to the phrase. Being "prepared to march," must mean more than just being mentally and emotionally prepared. It also means being *physically* prepared. Now I understand that using our *whole* selves—mentally, emotionally, physically—is a form of worship, for connecting Body, Mind, and Emotions involves the Spiritual Values of Truth, Love, Change, and Harmony, and these bring us closer to God.

SPIRITUAL POWER LIES IN OUR RESPONSES

When you are REAL, you are empowered, and when you unite these vital aspects of yourself and reflect the Spiritual Values through this unity, you can come to a new understanding of spiritual responsibility. Many people think of responsibility as being accountable, like paying the bills, or owning a mistake, or performing a duty. When I talk about responsibility, I'm talking about *Response-Ability*—the ability to respond mentally, emotionally, or physically to a situation.

If you were taught that some part of yourself is unacceptable, you probably tried to change or discard it in order to be accepted. Often people reject their hostile feelings and sexuality—parts frequently labeled "dark" or "evil." Some religions, especially Christianity, pit the so-called good or light sides of humanity against the dark forces, and teach us to try to remove or avoid these supposedly bad feelings, thoughts, or behaviors.

But if you abandon, sublimate, or disown some aspect of yourself, physically, emotionally or mentally, you are limiting your ability to fully respond, diminishing your spiritual power. Have you ever had a lamp that had an old or damaged electrical cord? The lamp works, but not at full power. Similarly, your spirituality cannot shine brightly when you cut the energizing connection between body, mind and emotions. You cannot fully respond to—or connect with—God when you are separated from yourself, because when you disconnect from yourself, you disconnect from God.

Spirituality's Transforming Power

Spiritual teachings are not consistent on the issue of what to do with our dark or shadow sides—the parts of ourselves that have been damaged or wounded or which simply reflect negative aspects. Most advocate abandoning or overcoming this side of being human. I believe the reason so many people are drawn to metaphysics or Native American spirituality is the way these teachings of universal principles lead to an understanding of harmony: the duality of our nature is seen not in terms of good or bad, one valued, the other to be avoided or removed. Instead, native or shamanic religions teach that we must learn to embrace or transform these energies to achieve a balance (the Spiritual Value of Harmony). In his book, *Earth Medicine*, Kenneth Meadows writes:

> American Indian traditions were based not on a set of beliefs or on any interpretation of sacred writings, but on the knowledge of the pulsating rhythm of life that could be seen and sensed all around . . . Earth medicine shows up our personality blemishes as well as our strengths so that we may do something about them, too. And Earth Medicine indicates where to look, to remove the blemishes that cause us so many problems in life.[3]

I like this description because it emphasizes some important aspects of my understanding of spirituality. It illustrates how all of life is connected, as well as providing a different context in which to view the negative parts of life. I can see why many people would be drawn to the Native American understanding of what was traditionally called "sinful" as natural energies that can be understood and controlled, because it frees people of shame and guilt and opens the door to change. It also incorporates the idea of balance and acceptance of our whole person, while still addressing aspects of ourselves we want to change. Personally, I can deal with having a blemish, as opposed to being told I am inherently a blight. In many ways, this Native American belief mirrors something I talk about often: that people don't always know the difference between *making* a mistake and *being* the mistake.

Also, this description echoes one of my own guidelines to creating healthy spirituality, which is that our beliefs must make sense. Some people are attracted to metaphysics and shamanism because those disciplines seem to offer an understanding of human nature and our relationship to the world that makes sense. If we were not created to be perfect, then our imperfections need not imply that we are defective, damaged goods. As the saying goes, "God does not make junk." We were designed with the ability to creatively live with those imperfections. This is how we involve God in our lives, in the ways in which we deal with those things the great Roman Catholic theologian Teilhard de Chardin called "diminishments."

A healthy understanding of spirituality enables you to balance these imperfections, these polarities. Healthy spirituality empowers you to deal with (and transform) your Shadow side instead of denying it altogether. You must learn to examine, embrace, even befriend your imperfections, or else you will never find spiritual balance.

The Transformation process employs all the Spiritual Values of Truth, Love, Change, and Harmony. I talked earlier of my nervous stutter, and the facade I built to cover it. My stutter never entirely vanished. It still pops up when I am tired, or excited and energized about something, or am feeling emotional. Today, I'm no longer ashamed of my stutter. Sometimes, I actually employ it in my talks and lectures when I want to inject some humor or lightness. I actually *use* it to make a point. It can also serve as a signal to me: "Leo, you're tired. Leo, what are you feeling? Are you afraid? Are you lonely?" Its presence connects me with my younger self and reminds me of who I was and am. Like Rudolph the red-nosed Reindeer, I'm learning to turn my liabilities into assets. I'm using what was once seen as a defect in a positive and creative way, and this opens the door to many spiritually powerful moves.

In the old days, I tried my best to transcend—to rise above—my physical and emotional self. As an Anglo-Catholic, I was as close to being Roman Catholic as I could get and still be a Protestant. While I didn't agree with the Catholic Church on the issue of chastity and birth control, I had absorbed a lot of the Jesuit attitudes toward the body and toward women. It was easier to solve the conflict by numbing out with alcohol and religious dogma than it was to reconcile the conflicts that raged between my body, mind, and emotions. As I said earlier, I tried to transcend my human desires and failed miserably. The more I "transcended," the more unpleasant I became to everyone, including God.

Today, I prefer to be a different Leo. I prefer to be able to say to my congregation, "I don't know" instead of having to have all the answers. I'd rather empower myself by talking to bank officers (something I *don't* enjoy!) than become a victim of my own fears. When I stopped trying to transcend, overcome, or remove my negative qualities, and instead began to work on *transforming* them, I discovered a greater connection to God. Now I have a more powerful relationship with God than I have ever known. Today, my relationship with God is reflected in the choices I make and the process I use to make them. I manifest my spiritual power not by sitting and waiting passively for God to do something, but by calling on my God-given resources and creating a partnership with God.

When I use the transformative qualities of spirituality to unite Body, Mind, and Emotions, and through that unity reflect the Spiritual Values of Truth, Love, Change, and Harmony, I reach that place of spiritual grace I call *At-ONE-Ment*. I am at one with myself, with God, and with the world. Being "At-ONE" doesn't mean there's no pain or that no problems plague me. What it means is that I face them in spiritual peace assured that no matter the outcome I can and will walk through the pain and fear. I no longer have to focus my energy on enticing God into my life as a reward for good behavior. I know God is with me no matter what. It is through the grace of "At-ONE-Ment" that I have come to a new understanding of what it means to "rest in God." When I am at one with myself, I am better equipped to be at one with other people, and my world, and this interconnectedness brings me even closer to God.

Perhaps you are like me. Perhaps you are ready to discover that you've been connecting with God in many places and using your spiritual power without knowing it. I hope that coming to a new understanding of spirituality and its place in your life will help you to answer some of your questions about spirituality. Coming to a new understanding of spirituality can transform every aspect of your life and relationships, not only with God, but at work, play, and with your family. It can expand your sense of worship to embrace and unify religious life, cultural heritage, and ecological concerns. Perhaps it will also help you recognize that you can stop trying to "get" spiritual, because you've really been spiritual all along!

NOTES

1. "It is all a process of change . . ." Ywahoo, Dhyani. *Voices of Our Ancestors: Cherokee Teachings from the Wisdom Fire.* (Boston: Shambhala Publications, Inc. 1987). p. 258.

2. "What is REAL . . ." Williams, Margery. *The Velveteen Rabbit.* (New York: Avon Books, 1985). pp. 12-13.

3. "American Indian traditions . . ." Meadows, Kenneth. *Earth Medicine: A Shamanic Way to Self Discovery.* (Longmead, England: Element Books, 1989). pp. 9-14.

2

Coming to a New Understanding of God

> Father Leo, I love how you talk about a new under-
> standing of God. But how do I get that? I've tried dif-
> ferent religions, but it didn't really change anything. I
> still feel like a pawn God or the Universe just plays
> with, like I don't really matter. What's wrong with
> me? How can I change how I feel about God?
>
> *Joe S.*

AT WORKSHOPS, IN LETTERS OR PHONE CALLS TO MY OFFICE, IN PSY-
chiatric centers where I work with patients, or at churches where I have
spoken, people ask me the same questions: *I keep trying to come to a new
understanding of God, but I never seem to make it work . . . Why can't I feel comfortable with God?*

Those who search for a different understanding of God often don't
have a clear idea of what a different understanding would mean.
Usually, they think it is a particular church or philosophy which isn't
working for them, so they wander through a variety of churches or
belief systems, dragging their same old beliefs about God with them.
They don't realize that the religion often isn't the real problem. It's their
Core Beliefs about God—which remain constant—that create the pain.

How you see God molds you into certain patterns, and shapes who
you are. Your relationship with God is determined by what you believe

about God—what your image of God is like. And these deeply embedded Core Beliefs about God probably began in childhood. While you
may, on a conscious level, seek a new philosophy or understanding of
God, those ingrained beliefs about God remain as the foundation of
your belief system and may be inhibiting you from taking responsibility for changing your relationship with God. Changing religions without
changing Core Beliefs is like packing your laundry in a new suitcase—
you're still carrying around the same old stuff.

In order to make real changes, you need to clearly identify what it is
you're trying to change. Most importantly, you need to feel free to make
those changes. Change involves taking a new direction, shifting attitudes,
being willing to do things differently—taking risks. Empowerment is
knowing that you are allowed to change, and making the moves to effect
changes.

In God's Image:
How Our Concept of God Molds Us

I grew up being taught I was a child of God. I'm sixty-three
years old, and I'm so co-dependent it damn near killed me. I'm a
grandmother, but everywhere I went—my church, even A.A.—
they kept telling me to rely on God like I was still a little girl.
Nobody ever taught me how to have a grown-up relationship
with God!

Janice

Our image of God begins in childhood. It grows out of what we are
taught at home or in our religion. It is also shaped by the society and culture in which we live, so that even those who grow up in a non-religious
family can acquire an image of God that is reflected through their culture or ethnic heritage. Our cultures and societies often reflect the prevailing religious heritage. Thus, many European, Mediterranean, and
South American cultures reflect the staunch patriarchy and authoritarianism of the Early and Medieval Catholic Church. American society
was shaped by the dominant Protestantism of its founders. Asian and
Indian cultures reflect the Hindu and Buddhist belief systems; the
Middle East is influenced by Islamic and Judaic customs. Our cultural

heritage alone, divested of any specific religious teachings, can shape our world-view and alongside that, our image of God.

But most people gain their image of God from their families. I wrote earlier about how the religious arguments between my parents formed my own childhood image of God. As a child, I was taught to fear God. As a teenager, I feared God yet desperately wanted to love God. Unable to resolve the conflict between my childhood image of God and the yearning I felt for a sense of safety and nurturing in God's arms, I fell in love instead with the power, control and majesty of the church. Although I didn't know it, the Church became my substitute for that God who so confused and frightened me.

Former nun Karen Armstrong writes in her introduction to *A History of God,*

> My ideas about God were formed in childhood and did not keep abreast of my growing knowledge in other disciplines. I had revised simplistic childhood views of Father Christmas; I had come to a more mature understanding of the complexities of the human predicament than had been possible in kindergarten. Yet my early, confused ideas about God had not been modified or developed. People without my peculiarly religious background may also find that their notion of God was formed in infancy.[1]

Some of the most telling examples of how children see God come from a little book called *Children's Letters To God.*[2] As I read through it, I was alternately amused, saddened, and awed by the hopes, fears and insights expressed by these young children of God.

One letter read:

Dear God,
    It rained for are whole vacation and is my father mad! He said some things about you that people are not supposed to say but I hope you will not hurt him anyway.

Your friend
    But I am not going to tell you who I am.

In other letters, sexual fear rears its head:

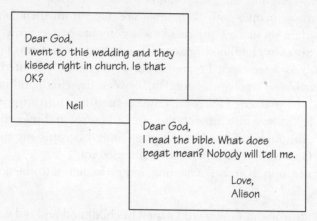

Dear God,
I went to this wedding and they
kissed right in church. Is that
OK?

Neil

Dear God,
I read the bible. What does
begat mean? Nobody will tell me.

Love,
Alison

Then there are the letters to "Santa God:"

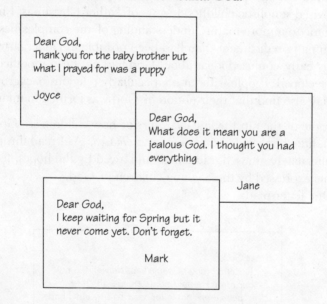

Dear God,
Thank you for the baby brother but
what I prayed for was a puppy

Joyce

Dear God,
What does it mean you are a
jealous God. I thought you had
everything

Jane

Dear God,
I keep waiting for Spring but it
never come yet. Don't forget.

Mark

These letters reveal how children absorb the information that is given to them. The assumption is that children outgrow such confusion, but I don't think that's so. As I read through the letters, I wondered over and over, did anyone ever sit down with those children and answer their questions? Some of them were mighty important questions: *"How did you know you were God? How come you did all those miracles in the old days and don't do any now? Instead of letting people die and having to make new ones, why don't you just keep the ones you got now?* I wonder if the parents of these children ever heard those questions, and more important, what kind of answers did they give? What happened to these children's fears, confusion, and suggestions to God about how to improve their world?

My experience tells me that when these children reach adulthood their questions will remain, in one form or another, unanswered and unexplained—their fear, confusion, and concern as fresh as it was when they wrote their letters to God. The belief that God will punish the father who curses about a rained-out vacation, the idea that God will send puppies, the fear that kissing in church might not be OK, the puzzlement over what God has to be jealous over, and the fear that God might forget to send the spring—these linger on into adulthood, and remain at the core of the image of, and relationship with, God.

I have met and heard about many people who made a conscious effort to change their understanding of God, mostly by changing religions or leaving religion altogether. No matter which path they take, their actions and attitudes toward themselves and other people are still determined not by their new beliefs, but by the image of God they developed in childhood.

JANE'S STORY

I'm a "recovering Catholic." I've been saying that for years, thinking I'd really recovered, but something happened recently that makes me wonder.

When I was growing up, I don't know who I hated more: myself, the Church, or God. We had a lot of rules in our house, and most of them were about not making people mad, especially my father. It's weird, because I don't recall Dad ever getting violent or yelling, but from the time I was real little, I remember Mom being absolutely terrified we'd do something to make him mad. It was against the rules in our house to ever hurt anybody's feelings or do something that even looked like it might be selfish. If we did, we'd have to go to our rooms and say the Rosary or the Hail Mary over and over again, and then do some kind of chore as an extra penance.

It was just as bad at school. I used to think Mom was in

cahoots with the nuns, because we got the same thing there, only the nuns were a whole lot more explicit about what would happen if we made God mad. I couldn't wait to grow up and get away from it. But I didn't dare show how I felt. I always put on a "nice little girl" front, but inside I was just boiling over with rage. I couldn't wait to grow up and get away from there.

I got into Yoga and Eastern meditation when I was in college. I've been working with it for over ten years now. It really helps me settle down when I feel anxious or upset about something, and I've felt good about putting all that angry Catholic stuff behind me.

Something happened recently that's got me really confused. I got promoted at work to a supervisor's position, which is something I've worked towards for a long time. I had to make some decisions about the schedules that some people didn't like and there was a big confrontation with one of my co-workers. I was so bummed and upset when I got home, I went straight to my room and lit incense and meditated for hours. When I came out my roommate said, "Gosh, Jane, wouldn't it be easier to say three Hail Mary's and be done with it?"

It blew me away to realize I'm still doing the same thing I hated having to do when I was a kid. I thought I'd gotten away from it a long time ago. My roommate says she noticed it right away. She was raised Catholic, too, so it wasn't hard for her to spot it. I've probably been "doing penances" with my meditation all along. But now I'm almost scared to meditate. I feel kind of lost now, and I'm not sure why.

Jane's story is typical of many that I receive. Jane thought she'd moved away from the fear-based belief system in which she had been raised. Yes, she changed religions, but her Core Beliefs remained intact: She shouldn't make anyone mad, and if she did, she should do penance to avoid further punishment. I suggested to Jane that she get some help from a therapist for her co-dependency and adult child issues. When I heard from her again, she was pleased to report that she had gained some deep insights into the roots of her co-dependency, and she had started meditating again. "Only now I meditate to affirm my power and get centered when I feel off-base. And I really feel more connected to God than I ever did before!" she wrote excitedly.

WE ARE WHAT WE BELIEVE

Jane's experience illustrates another important point about our Core Beliefs: What we believe about God, we become. Jane believed in a "punishing" God. She believed that she would be punished for being herself—that was "bad"—and whenever she was "bad" she "did penance" (punished herself).

Likewise, if we believe in an angry, judging God, we will become angry and judging. If we believe in a God who is a Fixer-Rescuer, we will become passive and dependent, always needing to rescue or be rescued. I believed in a distant God, one who was buffered by the Church, accessible only through rituals and prayers. So it is not surprising that in those days I could only feel close to other people through shared activities—drinking, theater, retreats. I had friends, but always kept them at a distance. I played out my relationship with God in my relationships with other people, including myself.

The truth was I did not *want* a close relationship with God, because that would have taken me too close to the scary "bogeyman" God of my childhood—the one who, as I saw it, caused my parents to quarrel and fight so viciously—the God who was tearing apart my home. I didn't understand *that* God. I was afraid of that God. I didn't comprehend then that the real God, the God I would eventually have a positive relationship with, was the exact *opposite* of that God. This truly was the dysfunctional God concept that was destroying not only my home, but my spiritual empowerment. But back then I couldn't easily divorce myself from the scary God of my childhood, so I put religion and the priesthood between us, just as religion and the priesthood stood between me and my other relationships.

In order to change, I had to come to a new understanding of God. To do that, I had to confront that bogeyman God. I had to help little Leo creep out from under the covers and really look at the image of God the adult Leo had carried from childhood. I had to identify the messages about God that I'd harbored since childhood, and look to see how they affected my life. Perhaps you will recognize some of the same messages that helped create your own image of God in these concepts of God that I changed.

Some Concepts of God that I Changed

WAITING FOR GOD TO MAKE THE FIRST MOVE

I can't remember how old I was when my parents first started drilling into me that God had all the power in my house. It wasn't just the arguments. If there was anything my mother wanted to have changed, she would announce that she was "praying about it." All during my drinking years, she would pray daily to the Virgin Mary to have God make me stop drinking. For over fifteen years now, my mother has heard me lecture, she has read my books, attended my "Say Yes To Life" Conference Cruises, and still in her heart of hearts, she believes that the Virgin Mary answered her prayer. If I were still being driven by my childhood image of God, I'd be one of those who gets up and says "God got me sober." And my mother would undoubtedly be smiling smugly, very proud that her prayers had done the trick.

Today, I believe that *God made the first move* by giving us the freedom to think, reason and choose. But from there on, the moves are up to us. We can remain passive, waiting for God to make more moves, or we can activate a co-creatorship with God by choosing what to do with our abilities.

For example, recently I met with a mission leader from the Diocese whom I had invited to help us organize an ongoing stewardship project. We talked about various strategies and approaches, then he leaned back and said, "You know Father Leo, if we'd just get out of God's way, the church would grow." Needless to say, my jaw dropped and I was actually speechless. I'd heard the same theme expressed in New Age churches and Twelve Step support groups, but I'd never heard it from an Episcopal missionary.

"You mean, if we stop getting in the way—whatever that means— then God would have free rein to work a miracle for my church?" I asked.

"Without a doubt," he replied. Rather than challenge him then, I decided to see where he would go with this. He immediately launched into a barrage of questions: Did we have a mission statement? Who were my key players? Did we have a complete financial statement and up-to-date membership lists? He continued on in that vein before he noticed I was just staring at him questioningly.

"Why?" I asked gently. "Why do we need any of those things? I thought you were going to tell me how to get my congregation out of God's way so He can get to work answering our prayers."

He blinked as only an Episcopalian can blink when placed in an uncomfortable situation. "Uh, well I didn't mean . . . "

Sadly though, I think he *did* mean it. He was repeating back what had been fed to him in so many ways. This is where some of the conflicts come up that often confuse people. On one hand, we're told to "get out of the way and let God do it." Often at the same time, we are handed a list of things to do, and it's often not clear whether these are designed to keep us busy so we're "out of God's way," or whether they are intended as the footwork we need to do if God is going to "help those who help themselves." I don't think either view helps us discover our spiritual power, because each seems to imply that God needs to be somehow induced to make a move. Today, I believe that God works *with* me and *through* me, instead of doing things *to* me or *for* me. In that difference lies true spiritual power and a deeper relationship with God.

BELIEVING THAT THINGS HAPPEN ACCORDING TO GOD'S PLAN, OR "IN GOD'S TIME"

From early childhood on, I remember my mother saying things like, "If God wants you to have it, you will." Although we didn't call it "fate" or "God's Plan," it was clear that Mother thought God had an agenda for everybody. When people died, it was because God "called them home" or "their time had come." The same theme was carried out in my religious life. All the church litany, prayers, and sermons made it clear that God was "in charge." Even in terms of the priesthood, the message was that we should not question the "mind of God." Applications for university, requests for positions and transfers and other appointments were all made in the context of: "If God wants you to have it, you'll get it." Nobody ever seemed to doubt or question the logic; it was presented as part of the givenness of the human condition. When children died in infancy, we were told not to mourn because God wanted them to be His angels. I even heard it suggested that they were "too good" for this world. If that were so, then why were they born? Why undergo nine months in the womb and the difficult birth process if they were too good to be here? All grief and sadness were therefore buried behind the silent belief in a "mysterious God" whose ways are not our ways.

Today, I see the results of that buried sadness and anger. I hear the rage at workshops and conferences from people who were never allowed to question, to grieve, because "God knows best." I wonder how many people harbor a secret belief in a God that sits up in heaven with a big appointment book, checking off our individual dates with destiny. When I ask people what they mean when they say things are happening according to God's Plan, or in God's Time, they suddenly start stammering and hedging. In workshops I often ask people to draw a picture of what God's Time looks like. Is it a huge clock like Big Ben? Is it a twenty-four hour clock? How does God measure time? Is God in charge of our lives like some Cosmic Bus Driver, chauffeuring us through life while we just sit back and enjoy the ride? More important, what are we supposed to be doing while we wait for God's Plan to unfold?

When I first began my recovery and was working on relinquishing my need to be in control and perfect, I often heard "Submit to God's will" and "It's not God's will for this to happen." Certainly, my ego needed an overhaul; I needed to learn the difference between imposing my will and control on a person or situation, and taking action based on my best inner assessment of what my choices and moves could be. The expression "Let Go and Let God" is a common slogan of many recovery groups, and I have certainly benefited from its use. To me, letting go means to stop trying to determine the outcome. It doesn't mean just passively sitting down and waiting for God to reveal the next stage of "The Plan."

When I really began to understand what Harry was telling me— about how I could change—I realized that no one could get me sober but me. My mother, my congregations, my Bishop, and my friends had all been on their knees for ages, praying for God to do something about my drinking. What if it hadn't been in God's Plan for me to get sober? Or was it in God's Plan for me to become an alcoholic in the first place? In any event, I realized that I had to do things differently. I began to relate to such secular sayings as, "If you want potatoes, pray for rain—but also buy a hoe!" I discovered new meaning in the saying, "Give a man a fish and he is fed for a day. Teach a man to fish, and he is fed for a lifetime." What I heard in those sayings is empowerment and co-creatorship. God did make the first move when we were created with the freedom to think and make choices. God's Plan for us is to think, to co-create, to be partners and players in the game of life. Otherwise, we truly do remain pawns in a Cosmic chess game.

USING PRAYERS, RITUALS AND RELIGIOUS PRACTICES TO INFLUENCE GOD'S PLAN

In his play "Shadowlands," author C.S. Lewis writes, "I pray not to change God, but to seek to change myself." I really related to that. I used to pray to tell God what was going on in my life—and what I wanted God to do about it. I think I used prayer to try to influence God to do something He was disinclined to do. And the more people involved in the prayer, the greater the chance of God hearing you. In my heady Anglo-Catholic days, I thought that the incense, candles, hymns, and elaborate vestments only helped in the spiritual coercion the church heaped on God. It was like groups of Christians all crowding around a megaphone shouting, "Now hear this, God. We need you to do something about South Africa, about AIDS, and the homeless in the parks. Now PLEASE do something—(if it's Your Will, of course.)" Yes, sometimes it seems to "work." In my playful moments, I imagine that the combined lung power of my mother, my congregations, and the Bishop made such a loud racket that God "let" me get sober just to get some peace and quiet!

Yes, this is a characterization to illustrate a point. And it's not meant to deny the power of prayer in our lives. One example of "powerful prayer" from the bible is the "shout" of the blind beggar Bartimaeus, who kept calling out to Jesus, even when the crowd around him told him to be quiet. In this story, Bartimaeus' shout was an affirmation of faith—it was a powerful move, not simply a plea for God to fix something. I see many congregations regularly beseeching God to resolve some conflict or problem, and doing nothing else. They ask God to feed the homeless, but they don't create or assist with a food bank or soup kitchen, or offer classes on how to write a resume or apply for a job. They want God to stop the drugs and gang violence, but from a distance. They don't want to get actively involved. This is the difference between a powerful shout and a helpless whimper.

Some people have an image of God sitting in the heavens watching over them. Unfortunately, that image often seems to exist alongside the concept of the judgmental God who is going to "get" us. Often, people who have an image of that God "upstairs" also think that prayer is about saying things to God, either in the form of requests, pleas, thanks, or adoration. For me, the idea of God "Up There" watching me gave me the shivers, as if God were sort of a Cosmic

Peeping Tom. That was my childhood Bogeyman God who kept tally of all my misdeeds and would come and punish me for them.

Today, I understand that God already knows what is going on in my life, because God is within me. So I don't need to inform God about events in my life, since God is right there, experiencing them with me. When I pray today, it is to deepen my relationship with that God Within so that I can discover what I need to do, what moves I need to make. This is a spiritually powerful use of prayer, for prayer has less to do with God's efforts and more to do with my own. Instead of asking God to do something for me, healthy prayer affirms to God and myself what actions I can take.

Viewing prayer as one of the means of communicating within a relationship opens the door to a number of ways I have come to pray. As I described above, there are the times I dialogue with God to discover what moves, what choices and decisions, I need to make. But I also practice what I call "Stillness" prayer. Have you ever known someone—a friend, or perhaps your spouse or partner—with whom you could communicate in absolute silence? You could be riding in a car together, each silent, enjoying the scenery, or sitting at home, reading or watching the TV; quiet, but still together and communicating within that silence. It is a wonderfully companionable silence, a state of attunement to each other that requires no words or even touch. I have such moments of companionship with God—driving in my car, flying in an airplane, taking a walk, or simply sitting in my home. These moments of still companionship are often impromptu; I usually don't set out to create them as I used to do when I would go on retreats to monasteries. In these "stillness prayers," I often find a decision confirmed, a feeling affirmed. For me, this is what "Be still, and know that I am God," is all about. It is a knowingness, a confirmation. Even though it is still, it is active, in the sense that it is about deepening and enhancing my relationship with God.

This is not "putting our lives in God's hands," and waiting for the outcome—what I call "passive prayer." There is a delightful Vietnamese story that illustrates this difference:

> A young man went daily to his fruit tree and lay beneath it with his mouth wide open. The gentle breezes stirred the tree, and the fruit would drop down into the young man's mouth. He loved his fruit tree for the way it dropped the fruit so abundantly to him.

One day, he went to the tree and lay down as usual with his mouth open, but nothing happened. The breezes did not blow, so no fruit fell. He lay there for many days, with his mouth open, and still, the winds did not blow the fruit down to him. He began to curse and cry, because the tree did not give him fruit.

A wise old man happened by and saw him lying there with his mouth open, crying and tantruming. "Whatever is the matter with you?" the old man said.

"I've been lying here for days, and my fruit tree will not drop her fruit, and I'm so hungry," cried the young man.

"Well then, why don't you just get up and shake the tree? Then you can get all the fruit you need!" exclaimed the old man.

So the young man got up and shook the tree, and sure enough, down came the fruit. And from that day forward, he stopped waiting for fruit to drop down, but instead, he shook the tree to get his fruit, and never went hungry again.

Active prayer is shaking the tree. That creates a partnership. Passive prayer is lying down and hoping a breeze will blow some fruit loose. It might work sometimes, but if you don't know how to get up and shake the tree, you could starve. And sometimes, the action becomes the prayer. Yes, I regularly dialogue with God about what moves I need to make. But then I have to "give my prayers feet." My church badly needs its roof repaired, and the congregation is not wealthy. We cannot sit with our mouths open and expect the Diocese to drop a new roof over our heads; we'd be in danger of getting mouthfuls of crumbled plaster and ceiling tile. We have held many fundraising events, and have had to "shake the tree" further by applying to the Diocese for a matching grant; meeting with the Bishop, providing the documentation of the work that needs to be done, the fundraising we've already done, and future plans. This is active prayer: dialogue, sometimes stillness and knowing, then action.

Making this shift to active prayer is an important move in the God Game. Not only does it strengthen a partnership with God, but it also helps you move away from the concept of God as a combination of Santa Claus and Houdini—the gift-giver/Magician who rewards you for good behavior or who can help you wriggle out of impossible situations.

As I described earlier, my personal concept of God was more one of God-as-Bogeyman. However, as a priest, I did my share of encouraging people's belief in the power of passive prayer and ritual as a means to attain grace. I'm sure that there was a large part of me that had subconsciously absorbed my mother's absolute certainty that God would indeed create a miracle if we asked long enough, hard enough, and through the correct channels. Yet at the same time, I think I was also secretly contemptuous of people who were so childishly submissive to that concept of God.

For me, the magic in my concept of God—the rush, the sense of awe, was largely produced by the orderliness of the rituals and routines. The prayers, meditations, rituals, monastic retreats offered easy solutions. If there was a problem, there was a prayer to go with it. If you did something wrong, you said three "Hail Mary's" and it was over. It was all very black-and-white, very tidy.

But this use of prayer and ritual did not teach me how to really get in touch with myself. It kept me from recognizing my feelings, and instead, provided a good way to escape my fear, my guilt, my loneliness. It took me farther away from *me* and just put more "things" between me and God. Moreover, it added to the confusion between magic and miracle. I tended to see miracles as happenings that occurred outside of myself, in sunsets, in beautiful works of art or theater, or in religious conversions or healings. Yes, I saw those things as examples of how God's creative power was manifested in the world and in other people. But I did not know how to see miracles within myself. I'm not artistic or musical, so I knew I wasn't likely to become the next Michelangelo or Mozart. That's probably why I loved Charlie Chaplin's Little Tramp. He seemed to be showing us how the "common man" could triumph. But my concept of God did not let me discover the "Charlie" in me—discover the many miracles that Leo Booth could produce in his own life. No wonder I chose a profession that had miracles built in so I wouldn't have to create my own.

Today, I do discover the small miracles within me. I have turned my gift for communicating into being a successful teacher, speaker and consultant on the subject of spirituality and addictions. Anyone who has ever taken the plunge and started their own business knows the myriad fears and risks attached to that. For me, the most amazing miracle is not that I took the risk, but that I came to a place where I believed I could do it. The Leo who relied on prayers, meditations, and rituals for guidance and power could never have imagined such a thing.

That's not to say that I don't pray, meditate, or take comfort in religious and spiritual writings. I haven't abandoned those things. Instead, I use them not to influence God's moves, but to discover and affirm my own moves through the choices I make. For instance, when I assumed the position of Parish Priest at St. George's Episcopal Church in Hawthorne, outside Los Angeles, I already knew I wanted to continue to hold a special service for people in recovery. At my previous church it had been celebrated as a special Mass. I had been concerned that using the Christian context of a Mass might prevent attendance by those who were not Christian or who had been turned off by religion altogether, and I very much wanted the service to be a safe place for people to discover healthy spirituality. So I changed the Mass to a non-denominational format and called it a "Celebration of Recovery."

After a couple of years of using that format, I began to see that it was not serving the function I had anticipated. First, the nucleus of people involved remained the same blend of members of my church and members of the recovering community who either attend other churches or are seeking a healthy religious/spiritual atmosphere. Also, and most important to me, I have remained a priest within the Episcopal Church in order to create a safe place to worship in a Christian context. I wasn't being true to myself or to my vision for my church by offering a non-denominational service, especially once other churches and groups began creating similar services. So after a good deal of soul-searching and dialogue with myself and others, I made the decision to return to a Recovery Mass format.

This is how I strengthen my co-creatorship with God, and energize the Spiritual Values within me. I had to get in touch with *me*, with how I felt. I had to check in with my own reality, my own Truth. It's how Choice frees me to explore options and discover new things. Knowing I'm not a prisoner of my choices allows me to change and grow.

Often, I'm asked about how to know when our choices are being determined by our egos, and when they're coming from our so-called "Higher" or "spiritual" self. The truth is, it's rarely that black-and-white. There's a danger inherent in compartmentalizing or labeling aspects of being human. Inevitably, it puts us at war with those parts that are labeled "good" or "Higher" and the parts labeled "bad," "Ego," or "Shadow." When those parts are all at war, nothing much can happen except chaos and the resulting shut-down of depression, or an abandonment of self that can lead to destructive behavior.

Yes, we will always make choices that are shaped by denial, by ego, by fear. The day we stop doing that is the day we cease being human. But when the time comes to look at the choices and actions we made, we can call on our Spiritual Value of Truth to help us confront our human desire to cover up, to deny, and instead, learn how to be honest with ourselves. If we repeat this process enough, I believe that in time, our choices will be more and more guided by the Spiritual Values, and less and less by the side of human nature that trips us up—the part that gets afraid, that craves approval, and wants not to be punished.

BELIEVING THAT GOD IS A FATHER
WHO WATCHES OVER HIS LITTLE CHILDREN

Probably no other concept of God causes such conflict and confusion as "God as Father," for this image of God is shaped not only by whatever religious teachings we may have received, but also by our experiences with our own fathers. I have found that people who had fairly positive experiences with their fathers have less trouble than those whose fathers were unavailable physically or emotionally.

In my case, my family life in many ways mirrored what the church was teaching me. Both of my parents are very humorous, witty people. And they both have hot tempers. But whereas my mother is outgoing and gregarious, Dad is more passive. He'll sit on the sidelines and make funny comments. When I was growing up, Mother clearly dominated the household. She made the rules; Dad reinforced them. He was the provider, the breadwinner, the supporter financially and emotionally of his wife and children. So when I'd hear about God the Father who would take care of his children, my image of "father" was one of passivity.

When I really got into the Church as a teenager, I saw the same kind of role model. Whereas Mother Church was active, controlling, and authoritative, God the Father seemed strangely passive and deafeningly quiet when you needed him. When you asked God for something in prayer, the Church replied, just as when I'd ask Dad if I could do something and he'd either tell me to ask Mum, or she'd just answer for him. I never doubted that God was there, but I seldom felt His presence. It seemed to me that even if God were not around, so long as the Church was, it wouldn't make much difference!

Many people grew up with the scary idea of God as some kind of all-powerful ogre who watches every thing little children do, just waiting to pounce and mete out some awful punishment. For those who also grew up with abusive fathers, the image of God as Father is likely to call up memories of beatings, put-downs, verbal abuse, and rage. And I have also met many people who, growing up with abusive fathers, created a fantasy image of God as the one who would come and take them away from the pain. These are the people who become perfectionistic, judgmental, controlling, and in a co-dependent rage because they could never get "good enough" for God to come and save them. Despite all their pleas and prayers, the beatings, the shame, the sexual abuse, the drinking, the pain, went on and on.

Janice's frustrated, "Nobody ever taught me how to have a grown-up relationship with God!" coincided with my increasing awareness of the great numbers of people I saw at conferences and workshops who had grown childishly dependent on their teddy bears or other cuddly objects. I was astonished to realize that several of my friends, whom I respect and admire, were far more intimate with their stuffed animals than they were with the real people in their lives. I have long advocated the use of inner child dialoguing and play to help people connect with their feelings, and overcome the shame ingrained into abused children. I think the use of dolls, stuffed animals, and other surrogates is an excellent tool for reaching and healing the wounded inner child. But I found myself growing impatient: What about the inner teenager ... the inner young adult ... the inner mature, responsible grown-up? How do they play? What do you have for them? In all the emphasis on reparenting, why weren't people being taught not only how to grow up, but how to live as a grown-up? Janice's statement hit me like a thunderbolt. Therapists are only recreating what religion has modeled: for centuries, religions, particularly Christianity, have perpetuated a childish dependence on God. The same mixed and confusing messages are there: pay your bills, but trust that your Higher Power is going to take care of you; be responsible adults, but obey God's rules about what to do and when to do it.

The more I looked at it, the more it made sense: What is "broken" in the relationship with God is the maturity of an adult partnership. A healthy relationship with God is an adult relationship in which God allows us to live our lives, make our mistakes, and take responsibility for them. As a little child of God, I am expected to sit on God's knee and be cuddled, protected, nurtured. As an adult child of God, I sit and talk with God about what I need to do, just as one talks things over with parents, sponsors, or other mentors. "These are my options; my decisions revolve around the following choices. This is what is troubling me; please listen as I sort it out."

As a little child of God, I was taught to trust in "God above," "God out there." As an adult child of God, I call on the power of the God within. Using the power of God within me—my God-given abilities—is what connects me to God "out there." I am still a child of God, just as I am still the child of my parents. But I am grown up now. In the Christian Bible there is a passage that says, "When I was a child, I spoke like a child, I thought like a child, I reasoned like a child; when I became a man, I gave up childish ways." Today, I reason with the mind of a man. God has given me a rite of passage. "It's time to grow up, Leo. Welcome to my world." For many years, I have closed some of my talks with a verse from one of my favorite songs, "Welcome to my world." I used it as an example of God welcoming us home. Today, I still believe that this is so, but it is the adult world of co-creatorship and partnership with God to which I am being welcomed—to which we are all welcomed.

My Concept of God Today

As a young priest, I preached that God was One, that God was beyond the Universe, and that God was Perfect Love, without ever really questioning what that meant. Today, I affirm that God is One, but discovered in many; God is beyond the Universe, yet within it; God is Perfect Love, yet embraces imperfection; God is the Divine Mystery, yet a deeply familiar guide and friend.

How did I arrive at this revised understanding of God? It began to evolve when I first started recovery. Attempting to detach my understanding of God from my religious doctrines, I made a list of spiritual values that were universal. Then I made a list of God-qualities—the qualities I attributed to God that I also recognized in other great spiritual and religious leaders. Guess what? They were the same. I use this exercise in many of my workshops because it really helps break through a lot of the "myths" and confusion about spirituality, and helps people start to formulate a new understanding of God.

God is alive in me. In the sense that we are ever-changing, and so always something of a mystery to ourselves, God is mysterious. God is a Mystery, and yet God is reflected and manifested in so many places. I don't have faith in just a mystery. I have faith in an historical understanding of God and life and what human beings can be. God is the living, visible link that connects Abraham, Moses, the prophets, Jesus, and the Apostle Paul with people like Charlie Chaplin, T.E. Lawrence, and Martin Luther King. God is my link with my fellow humans, ordinary people who are struggling with a faith in God and who are desperately seeking an understanding of themselves—just like me. Faith is my recognition and affirmation of my own link with the past, the present, and the future. Today, my faith is not built on the ethers, on the smoke wafting up from the incense that is carrying my prayers to God. My faith is *Real*, based on my current understanding of my world.

I believe that God has created a world that has its own energy. The nature of freedom involves the concept of paradox. The fusion of forces revealed in the universe, the world, and within human beings is diverse, independent, yet inter-connected. It is consistent, yet chaotic. Observable, yet sublime. We see the inconsistencies of nature reflected in human lives: healing and destruction, love and violence, birth and death. I find it impossible to give simple answers to the complicated questions raised by the universe, the earth, nature. Hurricanes, earthquakes, diseases, violence, prejudice, and fear exist alongside the magic of sunrises, the miracle of birth, the wonder of love, the majesty of human generosity and courage. It is all paradoxical and complex. But it reveals force. Energy. *Life*.

We achieve great things because we have greatness within us. We do monstrous things because we have our own Shadow within us. This is how we mirror the universe in which we live, the light and dark, destructive and creative. I am often asked nowadays if I believe that our own dark Shadow side is a reflection of the Shadow side of God, and if I think God has a "dark side."

To understand this concept, I had to be willing to move my image of "dark" and Shadow away from the negative meanings which are usually attached to them. I have come to understand the words "dark" and "Shadow" to mean that which is beneath the surface. So much of what is considered to be the human "dark side" has been buried in our pursuit to be pure. Our sexuality, anger, confusion, fears, imperfections are some examples of what many consider part of their own "Shadow" selves. These buried aspects often combine with each other and frequently seem to take on a life, an energy of their own. They can drive us, motivate us, without our being conscious of them, because we have sought to get rid of them. So they become part of our subconscious.

The God of our projection *does* have a dark side, because what we have *not* acknowledged, uncovered, embraced in ourselves, we have not acknowledged in our concept of God. So it also remains buried, unattainable to us as Godly or sacred. There's another way to look at how God could come to have a dark side. In *Care of the Soul*, author Thomas Moore suggests that we get our Shadow side because "the person we choose to be . . . automatically creates a dark double—the person we choose not to be."[3] Sadly, I think that most people actually believe more in the *God who dictates "who we choose not to be"*—the God who will punish, judge or reject us if we do not choose to adhere to a religious standard or ethic.

For the most part, I had created an English-gentleman type God, a distant, non-involved God. That's why most Christians are much happier with a transcendent, divine, angelic Jesus, rather than a Jesus who got angry, went to the toilet, had sexual feelings, and suffered on the cross. I could only come to understand a truer, more real God as I became more real and honest about who I am. Today, I understand that the "dark side" isn't "bad," but merely imperfect, incomplete. My dark side, the energies that remain buried beneath the surface are simply opportunities to be positive and creative waiting to be uncovered.

I used to think of God as a Bogeyman, a terrifying shadow that haunted and stalked me. Today, my concept of God has evolved into a loving and nurturing Friend that constantly radiates spiritual energy within the universe. God's love is *demonstrated beauty* that I can see and perceive all around, and through this experience I am energized.

Changing Your Concept of God

First, let me emphasize, *it is not always necessary to change your concept of God.* If your concept of God is working for you, if it fills you spiritually so that you are not yearning or searching for a different relationship with God, then you may not need—or want—to change your concept of God. If your beliefs about God help you connect to yourself mentally, emotionally, and physically, and allow you to be spiritually responsible, your concept of God is just fine.

Sometimes, we really don't have to abandon our concept of God, we just need to make a slight shift in our understanding of what our relationship to God can be like. Janice, for example, doesn't want to stop being a child of God. She just wants to have a grown-up relationship with God! Similarly, I did not abandon my understanding of the historical God of my religious beliefs. Instead, I had to re-evaluate the ways I used to access God. I had to see that the way I used ritual and prayer and meditation only served to keep God distant. I needed to discover new means of coming closer to God.

Yet I understand that because of the baggage that is attached to our beliefs about God, there is often great fear of changing our fundamental belief about God. More than one person has asked me, "Father Leo, what if you're wrong?" For me, the adventure of faith is that we cannot know absolutely. That's what makes the God Game so exciting! We cannot completely know God, for our human mind cannot encompass the totality, the infinity, of God. I believe that Jesus was not an ordinary man. In a unique and special way, Jesus had a "secular sacredness," a bigger chunk of that piece of divinity we all carry within us which made him capable of understanding the totality of God. Jesus could see more of the big picture. And it was in his *response* and *understanding* of who he was in relationship to God that reveals his sacredness.

Because our human minds cannot encompass infinity except in the most abstract form, we often use our spiritual creativity to find a container for God that makes sense—an image we can relate to. So God was said to appear within a burning bush, a rushing wind, or a still, small voice. Jesus often illustrated the Spiritual Values through the parables that drew from events in everyday life, so that people could relate to them. God is within the realm of *image*-ination. We reveal our own sacredness in our individual response to what we have imagined God is. So if we have a bunch of dysfunctional messages that shape our image of God, our response to God will be dysfunctional and limited. Our awe and wonder at God's mystery will be shrouded in fear and judgmentalism of ourselves and others.

So if you are not sure about changing your concept of God, ask yourself: Does my concept of God make sense? Does it fit the facts and realities of my life? Am I still carrying around my childhood image of God? Do I like the way my concept of God makes me feel about myself, other people, and God? Most important, are you willing to give yourself the freedom to explore a new concept of God? As I used to hear in my support group meetings, "Try a new way for a while. If you don't like it, you can always have your old one back!"

Coming to a new understanding of God, or even going through the process of examining what you really believe about God, holds the key to so much empowerment. For in this process, you will undoubtedly gain deeper insights into yourself and come to a deeper appreciation of your relationship with God, both as it is, and as it can be.

NOTES

1. "My ideas about God were formed . . ." Armstrong, Karen. *A History of God: The 4,000-Year Quest of Judaism, Christianity and Islam.* (New York, Alfred A. Knopf, 1993). p. *xix.*

2. "Dear God, it rained for are whole vacation . . ." Hample, Stuart and Marshall, Eric. *Children's Letters To God.* (New York: Workman Publishing, 1991).

3. "the person we choose to be . . ." Moore, Thomas. *Care of the Soul: A Guide For Cultivating Depth and Sacredness in Everyday Life.* (New York: HarperCollins Publishers, 1992). p. 16.

3

The Partnership of Religion and Spirituality

> Father Leo, at your workshop, you said we don't have
> to be religious to be spiritual. But what if I want to be
> spiritually healthy the way you showed us at the work-
> shop and still be religious? Is that possible?
>
> *Larry B.*

Yes, as I've often said, spirituality exists without religion,
but *healthy* religion cannot exist without spirituality. Without the
Spiritual Values of Truth, Love, Change and Harmony, religion disin-
tegrates into meaningless form. Spirituality is the lifeblood, the divine
oxygen that keeps religion healthy and allows it to become an energizing experience.

My own spiritual journey has been from a narrow, unhealthy religiosity to creating a religious environment that empowers spirituality. I
changed, and so can you, and I did it *without leaving the church*. I want to
see existing faiths and religions revitalized and spiritually healthy. I
work to realize my vision of a safe place that respects differences, diversity, and a basic "religious agnosticism" that allows for growth and
change. I use the term "religious agnosticism" to mean a detachment
from that "one-way only, we-have-all-the-answers" stance that seeds
religious abuse.

In *When God Becomes A Drug*, I discussed the dangers of unhealthy religion and religious abuse, and how to identify and begin recovering from them. The next step—which is the focus of this book—is to discover how to "spiritualize" religion—to imbue religion with the Spiritual Values of Truth, Love, Change, and Harmony. Then religion can provide a rich and rewarding setting in which to activate and realize our relationships with ourselves, with God, and with our world.

Yet I realize that not everyone has a desire to create a new understanding of religion. As with examining your concept of God, the important questions to ask yourself are, "Does my concept of religion work for me? Does it bring me closer to myself and all of my fellow humans, regardless of their religion, race or culture? Or does it allow me to only associate with people who share my specific beliefs, and exclude or avoid all others? Am I happy with that?" My experience of people who are extremely rigid and dogmatic is that they are constantly defending their positions, or are on the attack, trying to persuade others to their point of view. It is difficult to see the Spiritual Values reflected in such people. They often seem to be very unhappy or not to have any affinity for either their religion or God.

But I must also remind myself that not everyone who is rigid and dogmatic becomes intolerant and prejudiced, depressed and unhappy. Nor does it follow that everyone who hears about a new understanding of spirituality and religion will automatically want to make changes. Sometimes change must come gradually, evolving over a span of time. Because of my work with addictions and recovery, many people who come to my church aren't rooted in the Episcopal traditions. It is easier to introduce new formats because they aren't familiar with, or attached to, the older services and liturgies. I have a friend who has just assumed a position in a nearby church in which the membership has been established for many years. His congregation would rebel if he jumped in and began making changes right away. So his challenge is much different from mine in that he must gently and gradually lead them to a place where they want to do things differently.

If you have determined that your old concept of religion no longer works; if you are seeking a different understanding of the relationship between spirituality and religion, then you may find these ideas useful as you work to reclaim your spiritual power. You may not share my exact vision, but perhaps the suggestions made here will help you discover a religious relationship that works for you.

Because I am a Christian, Episcopal priest, my discussion and suggestions will necessarily be about the scripture and services of my faith. But I believe that the ideas I suggest can be utilized within any religion, philosophy, or belief system.

A New Understanding of Religion

I've often heard the saying that if you want to avoid arguments, don't talk about politics or religion. That maxim would certainly have made a difference in my childhood. Much has been written about why religion ignites such angry, intolerant passion. As I see it, there are two common beliefs about religion which seem to fuel most of the divisive and negative elements of religion: One is that religion is the infallible, indisputable Word of God; the other that there is only one "right" way to God and, therefore, to salvation.

If we can revise or detach from these beliefs, we can more easily create an environment that allows us to "spiritualize" religion so that it can become a healthy, vital aspect of our partnership with God. When we free religion from the shackles of "do-it-this-way-or-God-will-get-you," religion can offer us opportunities to make many exciting moves in the God Game.

RELIGION IS GOD-INSPIRED, BUT HUMAN DRIVEN

One of the most controversial and interesting aspects of God's revelation is what it means to say that the Holy Scriptures are God's Word. Some people believe that this means that they are literally and fundamentally the "exact" words and instructions of God. What it says is what it means! Many fundamentalists of all faiths—Jewish, Christian, Moslem, Buddhist—hold this position. But it is a very precarious one because it is built on a slippery mixture of rigid absolutism, myth, and magic that cannot stand up to close examination without falling apart.

Even in my most dogmatic Anglo-Catholic days, I never subscribed to the belief that the religious texts are the literal, absolute words of God, dictated verbatim to the various writers. First, there is the issue of language. Anyone who has ever struggled to translate one language to another knows that often words do not have exactly the same meaning in another language, or even in the same language. In 1994 most people understand the word "gay" as a euphemism for homosexuals. In 1894 the word "gay" meant happy or light-hearted. If I did not know this difference and I heard some describe my grandfather as a "gay blade," I would think he was a homosexual. I can't tell you how many startled looks I got when I first came to America and asked people for a "rubber" when I was filling out a form and made a mistake. In England, where I grew up, erasers are called rubbers. We have other names for condoms. So even in English, there are some crucial differences!

Then there is the human element. Have you ever played the game in which one person tells a story, and then the same story is whispered to everyone in the room until you come to the last person? Usually, when the last person tells the story, it bears little resemblance to its original version! So let's suppose, just for the moment, that God did indeed speak to Moses via that burning bush, and Moses did indeed carve God's actual words into stone tablets. The problem is, very few people could read and write in those days. Usually, specially trained people would write something for you, and you had to trust they did it correctly. Priests and rabbis would read things aloud, and give their interpretations of what they meant, and that interpretation would become part of the story. The next people to tell it would include their interpretation, so then you have two different sets of interpretations woven in and around the main story. Now imagine that this goes on for tens of hundreds of years before anyone starts collecting these stories and writing them down. The main story might still be in there, but it would be hard to figure out which parts were the original, and which parts were the interpretations. Under such conditions, a rigid, word-for-word adherence to scriptures is hazardous, because you really can't pin down exactly which words are God's, and which evolved out of changes in translation and interpretation.

However, like many other people, I believe that Scriptures of all major religions are the *inspired* teachings of God. They are a collection of writings, indeed, they are an entire library of books that contain historical narrative, literature, drama, poetry, creation myths, and allegories, which record how a certain culture viewed God. These writings reveal the history of a people's relationship to God—how they understood God's presence in the world and how this concept shaped their own interaction with the world as they knew it.

DISCOVERING SCRIPTURE AS
SCRIPTS FOR MOVES IN THE GOD GAME

What then is the function of religious texts? What is God's involvement in them if they are not the literal, actual Word of God, handed down to us so that we know what God wants us to do? Many people have been taught to see their religious scriptures as virtual prescriptions for living—spiritual medicine we take to cure what ails us. If we follow the prescription we'll be saved. No wonder there is often great fear and resistance to questioning scripture or changing our understanding of its message. We might not get well or be saved if we don't follow the directions exactly. But I find that people who see scriptures as this kind of "prescription" often get bogged down in the literal interpretations and end up missing opportunities to use it to enhance their lives.

No matter what religion you embrace, God comes ever more alive in scripture when you realize that *scriptures are a living record of responses and moves human beings have made in the God Game over thousands of years.*

Have you ever heard someone say, "You can write your own script"? In a sense, scripture is a whole series of scripts and dramas that illustrate many different relationships and ways to understand God. So the *Bible*, or the *Bhagavad-Gita*, or the *Koran*, or the *Torah* can be seen as instruction manuals—guidebooks to the moves we can make with God.

Scriptures show us how God has worked in, with, and through, humans from the beginning of time. Yet we must be mindful of the fact that imperfect human beings had the revelations; imperfect human beings wrote down and interpreted the stories that had been told orally by other imperfect humans for generations. Another key factor is change. What was believed yesterday is not always believed today. I suggest that precisely because of this imperfection, scriptures hold exciting lessons for us when we stop asking, "Did this event really happen? What does this really mean?" and start asking, "What can I learn from this story today?"

Does the miracle of the Israelites crossing the Red Sea really hinge on God parting the waters, or does it poetically and dramatically illustrate the faith and courage of persecuted people who made a powerful move when they stepped out into the Sea? How many of us, when the waters of our own lives have parted for us in new opportunities—a job, a house, a relationship—have fearfully held back and stayed on the banks? The "waters parted" for me when I was asked to move to

America to take a position as spiritual advisor to an alcoholism treatment program in Long Beach, California. My life would have been
very different today if I had chosen to stay safely in England. When I
was struggling to decide what to do, many stories like the one about the
Red Sea helped provide answers and offered comfort and hope. Even
today, it reminds me that crossing my own personal Red Sea didn't
necessarily guarantee me that I'd get to the Promised Land, or that life
would be full of milk and honey once I got there.

Thus, in many ways, scriptures can show us how a certain move
may play out before we make it. Scriptures become guides to an infi-
nite variety of choices and moves. We are not bound to follow just one
script, but rather, can "mix and match," can "write our own scripts" in
terms of the spiritual moves we make.

WHICH WAY IS THE RIGHT WAY?

Understanding the Scriptures as a guidebook to the many moves and
responses we can make in the God Game can also free us from the
necessity to be dogmatically absolute and right. I think the greatest
hazard in using scripture as a "prescription" is that it produces a liter-
alism and absolutism that virtually stops change and limits choice-
making. It causes people to try to squeeze themselves into a mold cast
by people who lived long ago, instead of teaching them how to draw
on historical experiences to enlighten and guide modern living.

One of the most exciting things about the God Game is that it
takes us out of a "win-lose" contest with God and puts us into a creative partnership that allows us to make choices and later, change our
minds and make new ones. It allows us to grow with the changes. So
this partnership can never be fixed or static.

Our responses change along with us. When I was a young man, I
experienced the Resurrection story largely through the drama and ritual of the church. I saw that the church, the "body" of Christ, had
come back "from the dead" after the days of despair and disappointment that followed the Crucifixion. But after I began recovering from
alcoholism, the Resurrection came to life for me as it never had before.
It was *my* life, *my* body, *my* priesthood that had come back to life,
renewed and revitalized. Which understanding of the Resurrection is
"right"? Both of them are, because both reflect the ways in which I
experience the Resurrection.

Similarly, let's look at the statement Jesus is quoted as having made to Peter, "Thou art Peter, and upon this rock I will build my church." For Catholics, this passage reflects the special status of Peter that forms the basis for the authority of the Pope. Peter himself is the focus. Protestants understand the "rock" to mean Peter's faith, which shifts the emphasis away from the personality of Peter and focuses more on the qualities of faith. This is one of the hotly contested ideas in the schism between Catholics and Protestants, and the cause of so much violence and hate. What happens if we look at the two views not from the standpoint of right or wrong, but as reflections of ways to experience God? Both are essential to the comprehension of the Truth. Rather than forming the dividing line between two opposing beliefs, the differing views can actually bring people together by providing insights into how they each experience God. With these insights, both can build bridges across their individual beliefs and thus create relationships based on understanding rather than opposition.

What About Sin?

I wrote extensively in *When God Becomes a Drug* about the damage resulting from the concept of sin, and I will explore its contributions to spiritual disempowerment later on. One of the biggest moves towards spiritualizing religion will be in revising the concept of sin to move it out of the shadows of shame and guilt, and into the light of a self-acceptance that grows from the Spiritual Values.

Most people see sin only in terms of the negative. However, it means more than something being bad, evil, and immoral. Sin is derived from a Greek word that means "to miss the mark." (You can see why it is important to have an historical understanding of scriptural origins!) The visual image that comes to mind is of an archer aiming his arrow and missing the bulls-eye. In a real sense, sin reminds us that we are not perfect. We are not God. But it is stretching this awareness to infer that being imperfect, that not being God, means that we are evil, bad, and immoral. "Missing the mark" simply becomes a description for missing an opportunity to bring Truth, Love, Change, or Harmony more directly into our lives—not because we are bad or evil, but simply because we aren't perfect; we can't "get it right" a hundred percent of the time.

Sin reminds us that we are incomplete. Sin is the grit in the oyster that becomes a pearl. It is the spiritual foundation of our restlessness; we are restless because we know we are not complete. If religion talks about sin only in terms of what we are not, rather than focusing on what we can be, what we can reach towards, then we will never understand spiritual empowerment. We need to remember that our own innate spirituality carried within each and every one of us is a given. It is the basis of our empowerment for it affords us opportunities to make our moves, to change, to grow. Our sense of missing the mark, of being incomplete, that angst at the core of our restlessness, only stimulates our creativity, encouraging us to reach beyond ourselves towards others and God.

Also, our sense of incompleteness allows us to live in harmony and understanding with other people. We are able to forgive and accept human frailty because we have experienced it in our own personal lives. Thus, a spiritually real understanding of sin allows for the creation of community. Knowing ourselves to be incomplete, we can become open to learning from the experiences of others without judgment and intolerance. A new understanding of sin forms the core of what it means to say, "Live and let live."

I imagine many of you now saying, "Yes, but Leo, what about rules? What about morality? What about laws?" In many cultures religion formed the basis and structure of government and societal laws. That is part of the historical and cultural heritage religion carries. But notice that here, too, religious laws have changed as societal laws have changed. The Apostle Paul commanded slaves to obey their masters, yet today slavery is repugnant and regarded as a "sin." Being enslaved to anything is generally viewed as a negative.

Such things as lying, stealing, raping, or murdering are widely regard as unacceptable by all religions and cultures, and probably always will be, because they violate the Spiritual Values. I think those activities are universally condemned. We may differ on the degree of condemnation, but I think we all agree that there are definitely some standards against which we measure certain kinds of behavior. The problems arise when some people try to control too much behavior, to impose rules and then attach God to them to be sure they are followed. This impinges on others' freedom to choose.

When you activate the Spiritual Values in your life and incorporate them with religious teachings, you get a spiritualized religion which can offer you guidelines to behavior without terrorizing you with shame, guilt, and threats of eternal damnation. When you make choices, encourage change, accept yourself and others, maintain honesty and reality, harmony and balance, you give yourself a healthy foundation from which to move about in the world.

Yes, there will always be those who are very wounded or damaged in some way, who are either incapable of making healthy choices because of some organic problem, or who simply choose to let their Shadow side run amok in the world. So of course, we need laws and standards and guidelines, but it is possible to infuse those laws with the Spiritual Values so that we as a global society do not become abusive.

RELIGION: THE TIE THAT BINDS

The word *religion* has its roots in the Latin word *religare* which means to bind. Later, it was applied to *religios*, or groups of people who shared similar beliefs. Religion is the glue that binds us together in a sense of community. What draws people to religion more than anything is a sense of belonging, of connectedness. Through holy scriptures, religion provides a means of connecting to our cultural past.

In *A History of God*, Karen Armstrong writes:

> Religion was a matter of cult and ritual rather than ideas; it was based on emotion, not on ideology or consciously adopted theory. This is not an unfamiliar attitude today. Many of the people who attend religious services in our own society are not interested in theology, want nothing too exotic and dislike the idea of change. They find that the established rituals provide them with a link with tradition and a sense of security. They do not expect brilliant ideas from the sermon and are disturbed by changes in the liturgy.[1]

Perhaps this explains why some people cling so furiously to the established rituals and understandings of a religion. They do not want to lose the sense of security and safety of being connected to a tradition and heritage. I've met many people who similarly resist giving up favorite family traditions. Yet much of religion offers a link with tradition. Armstrong also notes that humans have been creating ideas about God from the beginning and replacing those ideas when they no longer work.[2]

This illustrates a key point I have talked about before: Our beliefs about God must work for us, must make sense to us, in order for them to remain viable and vital in our lives. We cannot discover a sense of community in doctrines, dogmas, and rituals which have no relevance to our lives. I often see people in church wearing a superficial, brightly false "happy face." I imagine this mask covers the pain of being squeezed into an ancient mold which no longer fits, the pain of awareness that the religion is not working, doesn't make sense. Yet the fear of losing that connection to tradition and roots keeps people in denial of the reality, of the pain.

But when you incorporate the Spiritual Values with religion, religion can offer you that link to tradition, yet still be allowed to change. When you free it from the concrete belief that what was in the beginning must be forever the same, you can come to a new understanding of what religion can mean to you in your life. You needn't throw out or abandon religious ideas; rather, they become part of that body of scripture and cultural heritage upon which you can draw for guidance.

God, Spirituality, and Religion

When you Spiritualize religion, you make a dynamic move in the God Game.

Religion offers a vital connection to our heritage and, through that connection, a path to the future. At the same time, it is a means of connecting with ourselves, and with God. A good example of how this works occurred in my church recently. A member of my congregation, who I'll call Jeanne, attends a religious abuse support group that meets in my church. She told me about an insight she had gained concerning the formal church rituals and how she was finding new ways to discover them in her life. "I don't get anything out of the actual Eucharist any more and I've felt sort of sad and guilty about it." she said. "But then I realized that the feelings of support and connection I get from my support group make a kind of living Eucharist. I feel spiritually nourished from the sharing in my group. I always leave feeling more alive and connected to God."

For Jeanne, the shared blood, sweat, and tears of recovery from abuse serves the same purpose as the wine and wafers of the Eucharist. It creates the sense of communion and community that was originally intended in the ritual of the bread and wine. In this way she remains connected to her religious heritage while bringing it excitingly alive in her own life. Slowly, she is beginning to make the spiritual connection between what is symbolized in the Sunday Eucharist and the real life issues of community, growth, and support. In this connection the Body of Christ comes alive for her as it was intended in the ritual of wine and wafers. And in this way, she is making powerful moves in her own healing. Like Jeanne, you can bring religion out of mere form into a personal, moving experience.

In contrast, at Easter time, I went to a special anointing and rededication of all the priests in my Diocese. It was held in a church in West Hollywood. What a sight we must have presented to the homeless who huddled nearby as we all jumped out of our shiny BMWs, Hondas, and Buicks, garbed in our most stately ceremonial robes, standing about on the sidewalks on that warm spring day. We went into a dark church, heard a centuries-old Mass, received the routine communion, and poured out again to go off to a catered luncheon.

How different—and more spiritually meaningful—it would have been had we gone out into the neighborhoods and dispersed to feed the hungry or take food to the sick—something that would connect us to our communities.

Sometimes I think many clergy have simply become curators in God's museum—custodians of musty, antiquated rituals and rites that cannot bear the light of day, cannot be touched or handled except by the curator, keeping people *away* from God. I prefer to be the kind of guide who invites people to come and look, touch, see how it works, see how it evolved into things we use today.

When we take God out of the mothballs of dogma, ritual, *Bible* and Church, and begin to discover God "in the world"—in music, politics, social activism, literature, and nature—then we become revitalized. We are *experiencing* God in our everyday lives rather than limiting God to ecclesiastical history. Truth, Love, Change, and Harmony no longer become abstract concepts but real, living acts and moves that we make in the God Game. Until we make God real in our everyday lives we will never feel spiritual empowerment.

Spiritual empowerment is the realization that not only is God involved in our world, we are involved in God. To experience religion without this spiritual base is, in a tragic sense, to experience a religion without God.

Let me draw on an ongoing project within my church to illustrate how we can bring God and the Spiritual Values alive in our religion. My church is in a very culturally and economically mixed area in a community just outside of Los Angeles. Many members of my small congregation are unemployed or do not earn enough money to live on. One of the first things the congregation wanted to do was a to create a food bank to feed the hungry and homeless in our neighborhood, and among our own parishioners. Recently the secretary announced that the food bank had run out of food. This is how we brought the Spiritual Values to life as we approached the problem.

First, I had to accept the Truth of the situation. Flowers, choir rehearsals, and meetings with the Diocese to get the roof repaired are part of the "form" of church life, necessary but not totally vital. Feeding the hungry is not just a pretty story about loaves and fishes. It demands a committed effort, organization, time, and energy. It also demands cans of food and supplies. So I got on the phone and pulled together the committee that had been running the food bank. How did it happen that no one noticed the dwindling supplies until we ran out? Had someone been taking extra food? Or had the congregation gradually lost their enthusiasm for the project and stopped bringing donations?

It was clear that I needed to explore with my congregation the meaning of Love and how to activate it in our lives and within the church. Love is not just a concept we sing about in a hymn. It is demonstrated in our actions. I overheard a conversation between one of my church members and a homeless woman who was asking to work for food. The church member said to the woman, "I love you in Christ." The bag lady replied, "That's great, but I wish you'd love me less and feed me more." Protestations of Christian Love can so easily be a substitute for actually doing something. The *words* of Christian love offered by my church member may have filled some need in herself, but they weren't filling the hunger pangs in the homeless woman's belly. Love, like prayer, often demands feet, hands, a gentle hug—or a can of beans. We need to *demonstrate* our love in moves that strengthen not only the connections within ourselves, but to our world, for these are the ties that bind us to God.

The Spiritual Value of Change demanded that we look not only at how we organize and implement the food bank, but that I look at my part in shaping my congregation's awareness of the need to continue to bring donations to the bank. As the committee explored some of the problems, we noticed that sometimes we often have too much or too little of specific things—baby food and diapers, staple foods like rice and soup. So we resolved to try to keep a more balanced supply when we could. My first reaction was, "I need to have the chairman give me a weekly status report so that I can make sure to announce it during the service or have it in the bulletin if we need more of a specific kind of item."

Then I stepped back and realized that my part was more than the "form" of keeping the congregation informed of our needs. Here was an opportunity to help people connect the form and ritual of the service and scripture with everyday life. Many faiths call the ritual of the Eucharist "communion." It was meant to symbolize the Last Supper in which Christ broke bread with his disciples, and through that ritual, it became a symbol for our communion with God. In its early days Christians held the Eucharist in secret to avoid persecution and it became a special occasion for people who shared common bonds to come together.

Fortunately, today we do not need to keep the Eucharist a "secret" within the church. Just as Jeanne discovered a new way to bring the Eucharist alive in her life, the congregation of St. George's can discover new ways to "earth" the Eucharist through the services we provide to the community. Our food bank is also a Eucharist, a communion, a vehicle for bringing people together.

This is a move I made in the God Game: I want to be more than just a curator of religious antiquities, so I need to explore this understanding of Eucharist in my sermons, and work with the education teams to see how we can include it in the Sunday School lessons.

Our food bank also involves the Spiritual Value of Harmony. Again, it works beyond the logistics of managing this project. In order to keep it functioning well, individuals within my committee need to work together. They need to learn how to communicate with each other and how to work amidst differences in style and opinion. They also need to maintain not just balance of supplies, but balance of focus so that they don't lose sight of the "big picture."

But our food bank can also serve as another kind of vehicle for Harmony. When I first came to St. George's, it had a small side chapel that had long been in disuse, and had essentially become a storeroom. Because the community of Hawthorne contains a wide cultural diversity, there are many small Latino, Asian, and African churches that meet in malls, VFW Lodges, and other spaces. We decided we wanted to make our chapel available to one of these smaller groups who could not yet afford to own their own property. So there is now a Nigerian Assemblies of God church that meets on Sundays following our services (our parking situation doesn't allow both churches to meet at the same time). They are a separate church, a separate denomination, but since we share a building, we frequently host breakfasts and other events together so that our congregations can get to know each other. Since both of our congregations have many members who are struggling to make ends meet and are not able to spare much extra food or money, we've thought of asking the Nigerian church if they would like to join in some of our outreach projects like the food bank.

In this way, we can use the Spiritual Values not only to rejuvenate an aspect of our church life, but to build bridges within the community of Hawthorne, through our mutual efforts with the Nigerian church. Rather than opposing each other, which our very different doctrines might well cause us to do, we are united by the Spiritual Values in helping create healthy spirituality within the community of Hawthorne.

Discovering the Sacred in the Secular

By now, I hope you understand that I am not advocating an abandonment of traditional worship, but suggesting ways in which to bring our worship, our relationship with God, out into the world, into everyday life. For so long, the sacred has been locked up in the museum of religion. There are astounding miracles contained within the religious realm of the sacred: Michelangelo's awesome art in the Sistine Chapel, the majesty of the Cathedral of Notre Dame and the Taj Mahal, the glory of Handel's *Messiah,* the passion of the Hebrew *Kol Nidre,* the spectacle of thousands of Moslems stopping to bow to Mecca, the haunting dignity of Native Americans greeting the Four Directions at dawn. All of these connect us in many ways to God, absorb us in the mystery, wonder, and awe of our creative relationship with God. And they can bring a new awareness of Spirit, which is our ultimate *connection* with God, Higher Power, Great Mystery, Universe, Allah— whatever we want to call the Creative Force whose sparks reside within us. And the "New Trinity" that forms the basis of the connection to God is the connection of Body, Mind, and Emotions, of Mental, Emotional, and Physical. Whatever your concept of Spirit is, whatever form of religion you choose, they will remain mere empty concepts if you cannot integrate them fully in your life.

You can use your mind to understand, your emotions to feel, to relate, and your body to act, to make your moves. Do not allow religious taboos to think for you. When certain feelings and other aspects of yourself are banished to the realm of "bad," when your actions are bound by doctrine and dogma, then your ability to fully respond is diminished, and with it, your spiritual power. Similarly, if you limit where you look for spiritual inspiration to religion and holy scripture, to that small slice of life labeled as "sacred," you cut yourself off from a vast storehouse of spiritual energy.

Understanding the partnership of religion, God, and spirituality opens the doors of churches, synagogues, mosques, and temples so that the whole world becomes a house of worship. In this world, you no longer need to divide the sacred and secular, because all of life becomes sacred. The dictionary defines sacred as "being dear or special to a deity." If we understand that the Spiritual Values are the same as the God-Values, then we can see that wherever we connect to the Spirit, is sacred.

I have a Vietnamese friend who has taught me much about how to see life as sacred. Kien was one of my staff for many years. He is a Buddhist, and although he grew up amid the horror of the Vietnam war and came to this country as a boat person, he has retained the Buddhist sense of connectedness to all of nature. Often, he'd take the whole staff to the local Vietnamese shop to share some of his culture and heritage, and made it an adventure. For me, going shopping is usually just another chore, one of life's necessities. I go, pick out a plump piece of fruit or a juicy chicken, come home, prepare and enjoy it. "Ho hum. Good meal. Now on to other things." Kien makes the same process an exciting act of worship.

"Look at this lovely pear," he says, caressing it. He points out its rich color, invites you to touch it and admire its shape and texture. "Mmmm, smell how delicious!" he exclaims. He delighted in sharing food with us in the office. He would never just cut an apple, or dish up curry and plunk it on the table. Instead, he would invite us to touch, smell, marvel. He always arranged things so that they were pleasing to look at. In doing so, he brought us into the experience with him.

In a very real sense, without any of us being conscious of it, each time we shared a meal with Kien, we participated in a Eucharist, in an experience that connected us with each other and, through this connection, with God. Being four people of very diverse beliefs, we do not say a blessing—most of the time, we're lucky to be able to stop and eat amid the crunch of phone calls, project updates, and the pressing business of the day. Having known Kien gives new meaning to the expression, "being blessed" by someone's presence.

Through our expanded awareness of the sacredness of all things, we can discover new ways to create community. Already this new under-standing of community and relationship is allowing us to begin to con-front and change some of the problems facing us today. Many faiths are slowly changing their attitudes towards women, gays, and even those of other religions. In the last few years, I've been asked to present more workshops and lectures to a variety of churches, many of whom draw not just on Christian teachings, but on Buddhist, Native American, and meta-physics as well. These are not just New Age churches, but Christian churches like my own that are more focused on emphasizing and nurtur-ing the Spiritual Values rather than merely promoting a specific doctrine.

Being able to envision different concepts of God, spirituality, and religion that are free from dogma and "One-wayism" is often the first step to discovering what may be standing in the way of actually mak-ing the moves into these concepts. Clearing away the obstacles is not an easy task for many of them are deeply rooted and imbedded in our spiritual psyche. For years I despaired of ever being able to stop drink-ing. I had no hope, no clue as to how to go about it. You see, I knew the truth about Leo: I knew I was full of shit. But what I did not know was that I could change. Yet here I am, changed and changing. It's an incredible process—a dizzying, spine-tingling, stomach-lurching and altogether exhilarating ride with God. And it's only just begun!

Making the decision that you want to change—giving yourself per-mission to create a new understanding of God—is the most powerful move you can make. You cease to be a pawn and jump squarely into the adventure of the God Game. Whatever moves you make from now on will only nourish and strengthen your spiritual power.

NOTES

1. "Religion was a matter of cult and ritual . . ." Armstrong, Karen. *A History of God: The 4,000-Year Quest of Judaism, Christianity and Islam.* (New York, Alfred A. Knopf, 1993). pp. 91-92.

2. "Armstrong also notes that humans have been creating ideas . . ." Armstrong, p. 4.

4

Refugees From Religion

I have held my newborn children for the first time, oh, so close to my heart, but I did not find God.

I have walked the streets of America, my heart full of sadness for the homeless, the addicts, the battered women, and neglected children. And I did not find God. I saw the poor and barefoot children of Spain begging for food. Oh yes, there was a lot of religion in Franco's Spain, but I did not find God.

I have walked on the warm and sandy beaches, looking at the tumultuous raging sea, and I did not find God. I sat on the banks of the river, heard its murmur as it flowed to the sea, watched my reflection in its limpid waters, and I did not find God.

I kneeled and prayed in the little chapel of the town where I was born, and in the majestic cathedrals of Europe, confessing my sins, receiving communion from priests I despised, and I did not find God.

I have looked into hundreds of books, talked with the clergy, the teachers, the pious, the converted, the righteous, but I did not find God. I looked deep inside the inside of myself, and still I did not find God.

I have knocked at God's door so many times, but He did not answer. I would rather have heard Him say, "Go away, Marcella." At least I would have known that He was there. His presence has always eluded me.

Marcella S.

THEY ARE EVERYWHERE: FRUSTRATED, CONFUSED, ANGRY, SORROWFUL, or simply pathetically resigned. Some, like Marcella, search desperately for God in many places. Others want nothing to do with God. A few seek God in the more liberal mainstream religions; others have wandered into Eastern mysticism, metaphysics, or Native American shamanism. Some are merely adrift in the religion of their childhoods, not turned off enough to leave, but not connected either. They are the spiritually walking wounded: the refugees from religion.

They are fleeing a religious context that no longer makes sense, and perhaps never did. As children, they may have been physically, sexually, or emotionally abused, and somewhere along the line they turned to religion to escape or heal the pain. Perhaps they grew up with parents who were rigidly, dogmatically religious. Some were abused by religion in adulthood: those who were sexually seduced by clergymen, or the lonely, ill, and elderly who were exploited financially or emotionally. Often they are women who feel disenfranchised or unwelcome in many religious settings. Others belong to the increasingly embittered minorities—African-Americans, Hispanics, and Asians who find that their traditional beliefs and culture no longer provide comfort. Then there are those who are not totally comfortable with traditional religious teachings, but whose hunger for some kind of spiritual sustenance keeps them returning to what has become an increasingly empty religious table.

What sets these refugees from religion on their exodus? What makes religion seem unsafe? Why does religion no longer make sense? As we have discussed, spirituality is an activated, positive involvement that allows us to experience God in the choices and actions that we take to improve our personal lives and society. When spirituality is not active in religion, it is extremely difficult to create any kind of meaningful relationship or connection with God. People become refugees from this kind of spiritually-deadened religion.

One of the best descriptions of the emptiness of this kind of non-spiritual religion comes from former Catholic priest Arthur Melville. Melville's experiences as a priest in Guatemala led him to become a refugee from organized religion. In his book, *With Eyes To See* (Stillpoint Publishing, 1991), he describes what happens to our spirituality and our relationship with God when religion is missing the Spiritual Values.

My religious experience has taught me the importance of distinguishing between religion and spirituality, the former basically believed in or adhered to, and the latter primarily experienced. Not to make the distinction can lead to a repetitious, stifled, irresponsible life confused easily with service to God. Many religions with the original intent of leading to spiritual growth or harmony with Divine consciousness have come to make their structure, ritual, tradition and authority more important than the people whose consciousness they intended to influence. In doing so, they incite to conformity with a doctrine based on sin and fear of punishment—an unfortunate approach that, once believed, is eradicated only with difficulty. Such negative motivation inhibits creativity and freedom, qualities essential for harmony with the Divine.[1]

This priest experienced amongst the indigenous peoples of Guatemala the same kinds of spiritual pain and abuse I saw in my own congregations, and in the psychiatric hospitals, treatment programs, and recovering communities across America. We both saw people struggling to fit themselves into religious systems of doctrine and dogma that had no relevance in their lives, and suffering mightily for it.

What causes people to continue to try to fit themselves into one belief system after another? What impelled Marcella to seek God throughout Europe, in the sunsets and seashores, in the faces of her children, and in the depths of her own soul? Before we can discuss why the refugees continue to flee, perhaps we should explore what they are seeking to better understand why they cannot find it.

WE ARE RESTLESS 'TIL WE REST IN GOD

Perhaps you call it the divine spark, that little bit of divinity we each carry within us. Some people call it the soul. Others call it the enduring optimism of the human spirit. Whatever we call it, there dwells within us something that urges us forward, restless and hungry: the spark seeking the flame, our energy seeking its Source. No matter what image we use to visualize it, what we seek is connectedness—to ourselves, to our world, and, ultimately, to our Creator.

The philosopher Jean Houston divides human experience into three basic realms: the realm of THIS IS ME; the realm of WE ARE; and the realm of I AM. THIS IS ME is the level of the historical and factual, the realm of everyday life—birth, jobs, families, friends, death. Beyond that is the WE ARE, the realm of myth and archetype, sacred symbols and stories, the vast cosmic wealth of creativity and imagination, dreams and fantasy. The third realm is the I AM, or God—the ultimate Being with whom we all yearn to unite. As Houston describes it, we move through the WE ARE realm to reach the object of our deepest desire: the I AM realm.[2]

I like this description because it gives us a way to understand our restlessness and yearning, and provides some important clues as to why people often cannot use religion to create a healthy, empowered relationship with God. Our restlessness, our yearning, is essentially a need for affirmation and acceptance. We want to feel that when we approach God and say, "This is me," we will be welcomed and enfolded into the great I AM.

Religion works in the realm of the WE ARE. It is one of the ties that binds us and connects us to our historical heritage, to the sense of "This is me." That is why scripture, with its many books of literature, history, and drama, becomes so important to many people, for included in my definition of "scripture" are the myths and archetypes, the ancient stories which reveal so much about who we are both as individuals and as a species. It is in our nature to want to connect, to belong. Religion offers us a means to belong, both in the here and now, THIS IS ME level, and on the higher plane of being part of something bigger than we are.

Problems arise, however, because of three things: First, religion ceases to be a path to God when it becomes bounded by rules, dogma, and jargon. Instead it becomes a prison. Second, the allure of the WE ARE realm is that it also contains the intoxicating atmosphere of altered states reached through mysticism and shamanism, trance and transcendentalism. People often become so enchanted with this place of vision quests that they forget it is merely a stopping place on their journey, and instead settle down in this realm and go no further. Finally, there is the mistaken assumption that the healing of the soul which supposedly takes place when we unite with God will mean an end to pain and difficulty; that harmony with the Divine implies that there will be no discord in our lives. Somehow people have come to believe that "I will fear no evil, for thou art with me" is some kind of Divine Warranty against life's ups and downs.

But life does have ups and downs, light and dark, beauty and terror. A spiritually alive religion helps us move through those times. Indeed, all of the resources in that realm of the WE ARE ideally serve not to take us away from life, but to guide us through it. When we use prayer, meditation, rituals, stories, archetypes, and even therapy as a means to escape or remove some aspect of human experience, we ultimately miss our unifying connection with God. We end up in that kind of stifled, deadened life that Melville says is so easily confused with service to God.

But the kind of service to God perpetuated by a spiritually dead religion becomes not service to God, but mere submission and adherence to a religious structure. This was certainly true of me in the days of my religious abuse. The more rigidly I adhered to the form and structure of the Anglo-Catholicism I embraced, the greater the wedge I drove not only between myself and God, but between my congregations and God. I was more concerned with making sure I had a "full house" each Sunday, than with the mental, emotional, or physical condition of the people who filled that house. I scolded, browbeat, and shamed my congregations into forming and serving on numerous committees devoted to keeping the church grounds neatly landscaped, the vestments clean, flowers on the altar, births, deaths and marriages properly acknowledged. In order to avoid the displeasure of my Bishop, I threatened my congregations with *God's* displeasure if those service positions weren't performed well. Making my congregations responsible for these duties gave me more time to develop my alcoholism—it made a very good cover for a long time. It wasn't just service to God I wanted from my parishioners. It was service to *me!* Only in recent years have I come to understand that the congregation's anger that accompanied my leaving a parish was not just at me, for my alcoholism, but at God, for failing to deliver on promises I had made in God's name, most of which were under the guise of giving service to God and the parish.

I'm more deeply aware of the way most religious establishments have become estranged from the participating membership now that I am actively seeking to bring the Spiritual Values to life within my own church. My duties today as a Parish Priest involve more management skill and business knowledge than theology. I look at the operations of the larger churches, and see the ministers and associate ministers functioning more like the Boards of Directors and upper management of a huge corporation than as spiritual guides and caregivers. Against this setting, it's not surprising that worship and dogma no longer seem to relate to everyday life. Churches are too busy trying to keep the roofs over their heads (literally!) to really tackle the deep changes needed to ignite the Spiritual Values. Besides, if, as Karen Armstrong wrote in *A History of God*, people come to religion to maintain a sense of roots and connection to tradition, rocking the boat by changing the liturgy or evolving a new understanding of what religious traditions might mean today could alienate the parish—and the new roof still wouldn't get built.

Lacking the spiritually transforming quality of Change, religions are still relying on centuries-old doctrines, rituals, beliefs and interpretations. But when beliefs degenerate into mindless ritual, when structure crumbles into empty form, the debris that remains stands in the way of real spiritual experience. Instead the form, the ritual, becomes the only experience, and the connection to God withers and slowly dies. At this point, the refugees from religion pack up and move on, seeking a new place where spirituality is alive and vibrant. Perhaps this has happened to you.

Sadly, part of the structure of a spiritually dead religion is a belief system that implies that if the system isn't working for you, it's because something is wrong with *you*. You haven't prayed, meditated, or "practiced" correctly, or you have some inherent flaw that you've not "given to God" in whatever context that means. Perhaps you are a woman, trying to claim inner power and retain a sense of spiritual heritage not easily found in a patriarchal system. Maybe you are gay, or a survivor of abuse, or you simply want the freedom to create dialogue and be yourself, be real. For many of us, being told that we are "unacceptable" only fuels the deep spiritual yearning for acceptance, to really know that when we say to God, "this is me," we will be accepted and embraced. This is the core of Marcella's search for God—the hunger to know that God even knew she was there.

Who Are the Refugees From Religion?

Like other refugees, refugees from religion leave their original base for a variety of reasons. Women often become religious refugees because they feel disenfranchised from the male-dominated system. Gays are often literally exiled from the mainstream churches. Most refugees from religion are simply alienated and confused by religious and spiritual teachings which make no sense, or have no practical, demonstrable purpose in their lives.

Whatever the motivating factors, the refugees from religion usually fall into three categories:

Religious gypsies, who wander from religion to religion, trying to find one in which they feel accepted, one which ignites their spirituality.

Abandoners, who leave religion and remain suspicious and fearful of anything that smacks of religion.

Religious Ghosts, the spiritually disconnected who haunt our churches, New Thought congregations, support groups, and philosophical societies, neither receiving nor giving any spiritual energy. They participate in the form of rituals, but cannot move into *experience.*

Probably the saddest thing about the refugees from religion is that many of them do not know that they are refugees. Some don't have a clear understanding of what they are fleeing. Others don't really know what they are looking for. Equally sadly, many clergy don't know how to identify them, much less have any awareness of their issues or how to help them. They end up duplicating the same patterns that drove the refugees away in the first place, leaving them feeling more helpless and frustrated, angry at themselves, at religion, and at God.

Are you a religious refugee? Looking at each of these three types of refugees in more detail can help you identify aspects of your own attitude toward religion.

RELIGIOUS GYPSIES

These are the wanderers. Some prefer to remain in a Christian context, and so work their way through the mainstream and modern Christian churches. Others, unwilling or unable to move away from an organized structure, move away from the religious base of their childhood or culture and try it all: Buddhism, Hinduism, Judaism, Islam, Religious Science, Native American, Scientology. Often, what the religious gypsies are seeking is a sense of acceptance and belonging, which they gain through becoming the teachers and "servers," the movers and shakers in the religious communities. They often mistake the visibility and power they gain from their service within the church for genuine acceptance and spiritual power. They confuse the sense of belonging and being "part of" with that greater connection to the WE ARE Jean

Houston describes. Eventually, the emptiness of the form and structure causes things to cave in, and they come face to face once more with their spiritual disconnectedness and alienation from themselves, others and God.

When service to God is presented as total giving of self to the point that you have no identity, then you are no longer of service to God or to yourself, for you are no longer there. You become a robot, programmed to tithe, quote scripture, say prayers, chant, burn incense, go to services, revivals and retreats. Former priests Matthew Fox, James Kavanaugh, and Arthur Melville, as well as such authors as psychologists Joan Borysenko and Alice Miller all write eloquently about the loss of personhood this mindless service to God causes. Yet those who seek an identity in that service rarely recognize that they have lost themselves. Most of the time they think it is the structure, the context, which makes them feel lost. So they wander from religion to religion, seeking to find themselves, and instead, they lose themselves again by giving themselves totally up to the new faith or philosophy.

DAVID'S STORY

David grew up in a violently abusive home. His mother was a passive-aggressive co-dependent, his father was a mentally ill rage-aholic. When his father would abuse him, David's mother blamed him for it, saying he had somehow goaded his father into rage. His father had been raised Baptist, but so despised religion that he refused to allow his family to go to church. Wanting to be like other children, David tried sneaking off to church with his friends. He liked the sense of belonging and the secret thrill of getting back at Dad by going to church, until his father publicly abused and shamed him for disobeying.

As soon as he left home, David began his journey through many churches and philosophies. Part of him wanted to find again the sense of belonging he had felt so briefly as a boy; the other part wanted to become a "spiritual giant" so that he could get the best of his father. He tried Catholicism but it felt too "ordinary" and he wanted to feel superior, to impress people and be sought out.

David, as a result of his parents' behavior, is also very sensitive to criticism, to feeling judged. The slightest hint that someone has found fault with him sends him packing. He changes religions like other people change clothes, seeking to find the right place—a place where he won't ever be criticized. Recently, he started attending a New Age metaphysical church where he felt he would really stand out, and for a time, he did. He took all the classes and became one of the teachers. He quickly became adept at creating the metaphysical formulas that were supposed to help people connect with "Pure Spirit." He was told constantly that his varied religious experiences placed him "high above" most people spiritually—just what he wanted to hear. He gloried in the knowledge that the ministers and teachers were grooming him for high positions in the church.

Nonetheless, his religious experience was spiritually dead. Although his church presented wonderfully lofty ideas about freedom, love, and healing the planet, in reality, it practiced many double standards. While they offered many classes and seminars in active listening and meditation skills, they did not tolerate "active questioning" of their practices. The emphasis was on appearance and conformity.

In order to maintain the "high" of feeling accepted and valuable in his church, David positioned himself as a problem-solver. Although he has genuine skills at listening and guiding people to solutions, his manner is rigid and judgmental; he expects that everyone should want his so-called "superior spir-ituality," and lashes out at those who do not. David has a pecu-liar inner conflict. He wants to be sought out and consulted, but then he feels used and victimized when people *do* seek him out. He often speaks sarcastically and contemptuously, talking down to people as if they are children who just don't "get it." His relationships fall apart because he sees himself as a teacher, a trained listener, and no one else can communicate as well as he. Although he is very skilled at mediating and help-ing people confront each other, David himself refuses to be confronted. This attitude ultimately led to a fall from grace within his church.

During an oral exam for a counseling position within the church, David was confronted by one of the examiners. Having been told the exam would be conducted "gently and lovingly," David was caught off guard. His outraged reaction caused him to fail the examination—which sent shock-waves throughout the church. David was their prize student, and they were deeply embarrassed by his failure. His mentors and the ministers turned their backs on him, placing the blame solely on David.

Sadly, for all that this church and David himself prided themselves on being good communicators, neither the church officials nor David were ever able talk the situation through. David left the church, feeling unappreciated, victimized and now deeply, bitterly alienated from religion and from God.

I have met many people like David. They are often very charismatic, talented people. And very angry. They come into the church and immediately plunge into service—joining all kinds of committees and often gaining employment within the church. Only after I began to work with survivors of religious addiction and abuse did I begin to recognize the underlying alienation and lack of real people skills that usually accompany these refugees from religion. They come to religion seeking to connect, to belong, to feel accepted. They hurl themselves into the activities of the religious life, the classes, committees, choirs and organizational structure. They learn all the jargon, the forms of worship. Like the ministers in David's church, I have seen these "rising stars" come along, and even done my share of "grooming" and encouraging people to seek a higher station, without understanding just how alienated from God they are.

Today, I understand that it's not enough to train people how to perform this service or that duty. Learning all the prayers and liturgies will not help someone feel close to God who does not feel close to himself. David has many wonderful gifts, and his church lost someone who might have made a real difference in revitalizing and awakening the Spiritual Values within it. Both David and his church officials missed an opportunity to connect not on the level of form and structure, but on the deeper level of the Spiritual Values. *But the spiritually dead cannot heal the spiritually wounded.*

I recently had to confront one of my own "refugees," a person very much like David who seems genial and good humored, yet is underneath very angry. This anger often comes out in a variety of inappropriate remarks that are usually sexist or racist, or just plain judgmental and rude. Yet he is genuinely unaware of his own rage. He thinks he's a laid-back, easy-going guy, and doesn't hear himself explode. He hasn't a clue as to his own Truth, and doesn't understand that his happy-go-lucky front is a lie. Although I knew I was taking a risk by confronting him, that he might leave the church, I knew I could not allow him to continue serving in the position he was in unless he began to make some changes. Years ago, in the same situation, I would have sat him down, outlined his behavior and told him to shape up, and would have been satisfied with mere external changes. Now I recognize that I must help him understand how connecting in body, mind, and emotions can help him become more aware of what he is doing. He cannot change what he does not recognize. Today, I am more concerned that people learn to make the inner connections that lead to change, rather than with outward appearances.

THE ABANDONERS

There are some people for whom most of the traditional interpretations and structures make no sense, and indeed, are often offensive. These are the people who see quite clearly when religion is empty of the Spiritual Values. They may for a time have tried to discover a spiritually alive religion, and have given up in frustration and disgust. Sometimes, they have been told outright that they are not acceptable to religion or to God, and their rage is directed as much at the exclusion and rejection as it is at the emptiness. Many of the Abandoners have been Religious Gypsies for a time, and often are walking warehouses of religious and spiritual knowledge. They see how the religions connect, see the unity as well as the diversity. Many of the Abandoners believe that there are many paths to God, and no one religion has the "right way." Yet despite this apparent tolerance and acceptance, they are often intolerant and impatient with people who are religious. They are likely to see all religious people as hypocrites or potential abusers, or else pity them for being gullible or "led astray" by religion.

But underneath this smug impatience lies a very deep yearning for spiritual peace. Unable to create a relationship with God within a religious context, many struggle to develop a relationship with God that does not rely on formal prayer or meditation. Often, they will create their own ceremonies and rituals, being very careful not to "get religious" about it. It is often a lonely process, for setting themselves outside religion also sets them outside the sense of community and support which healthy religion can offer.

My friend Anna is one of the Abandoners. A recovering alcoholic and compulsive overeater, Anna is very supportive of me as an author and lecturer. Although she applauds my efforts at creating a spiritually safe place within my church, she has no interest in attending my services. "I don't do church," she says emphatically to anyone who invites her to a church, or church-sponsored function.

ANNA'S STORY

"I think I always scared my Sunday School teachers," Anna says. "I was always way ahead of everybody. I read the King James version of the *Bible* straight through a couple of times before I finished the second grade." Anna says her teachers were astonished not just that she could read the words, but that she understood the context. "From the very beginning, I was always questioning," she says. But one thing Anna never questioned out loud were the sexual taboos. "I think I was in third grade when I first started hearing that nasty phrase, 'Nice girls don't do that.' I'd cringe inside, because that meant I hadn't been a nice girl since I was five years old." Anna was sexually abused by a neighbor at age five. The dire threats and warnings about what happens to people who "aren't nice" became her secret torment. "I didn't dare let anybody get close to me. I couldn't let them know I wasn't nice."

As a lonely, isolated teenager, Anna often lay in bed a night, raging at God. "Why did you let that happen and then turn your back on me? It wasn't my fault. I was too little to know." Without ever really having heard the words lesbian or homosexual, Anna knew she was different, and had been all her life. She buried the secret of her sexuality, alongside her fear and guilt about the sexual abuse, under a wall of fat. "Nobody questioned why a 250 pound woman lived alone and didn't date!"

Interestingly, Anna grew up singing in choirs, and by her own admission, remains a "musical snob" when it comes to church music. "We had a really marvelous minister of music. I think he had five music degrees. Even though we were Presbyterians, our music was more 'high Church' than even the

Catholic and Episcopal churches in town." For Anna, music was her only connection to God in church. "I'd sit there fuming at the hypocrisy of it all, but the moment the music started, I felt close to God. The most spiritual experience I ever had was when I was about 12, and the concertmaster of the symphony was playing a solo. I listened to the sweetness of the violin, and the enormity of it hit me: God put music in the universe and gave us the ability to find it and create this incredibly beautiful piece. I was so blown away, I started to cry."

But music was her only connection with God in church. Increasingly, Anna found God in other places, and grew more angry and rebellious against religions that told her the "right" place to find God, and how "wrong" she was. It was this sense of having her own understanding and beliefs discounted and rejected that drove Anna away from religion. "No matter how much I tried to tell myself that it wasn't my fault, I couldn't stop feeling dirty and worthless, especially when I really started realizing I'm a lesbian," she says. "And how dare they judge me when they are so cruel and hypocritical!"

Anna is slowly rebuilding her concept of God from the ground up, even though she still holds religion at arm's length. Anna says that sadly, one of the biggest obstacles she faces in this process is that even some of her closest friends accuse her of not believing in a higher power or God because she does not attend a church or openly discuss her relationship with her God. "Yeah, to some extent, they're right. I don't get on my knees, or read my meditation books, or any of the other things I used to do. But that doesn't mean I have no higher power, that I'm not spiritual," she says. "I just say that my god is being remodeled, and I'm still looking at new designs," she laughs. But there is a real loneliness in abandoning the spiritual accessories which she utilized throughout her life. "I tried to find a way to use them healthily," she says. "But I kept making myself wrong—kept trying to make myself be the bad person. I finally had to accept that I wasn't wrong—the hymns and church services were!"

Anna has gone further than many people would consider, and her path is not for everyone. I receive many letters from people who are struggling to remain in some kind of mainstream religion, yet are experiencing great conflicts about the teachings and messages they are given. Because I have chosen to continue to serve as a parish priest, I receive many calls and letters from people who ask very deep, insightful theological questions about Christianity and the *Bible*, looking to me as a so-called "liberated priest" to give them answers. One woman wrote, "If I want to think of God as a woman, how can I still believe in the Trinity?" (Father, Son and Holy Ghost).

For other Abandoners, there are even more grievous problems. Many avoid virtually any contact with people whom they perceive as "religious." One man wrote, "I still cringe when I hear the words 'God' or 'church.' I get so angry, I want to choke that person. I don't want anybody around me who gets into that God stuff. I know I need to do something about my drinking, but I go nuts every time somebody says the word 'God' at an Alcoholics Anonymous meeting." In shutting himself off from God, in equating spirituality with religion, this man has also cut himself off from help. In his outraged abandonment of religion he remains a pawn—a hostage to the religious abuse of his past.

RELIGIOUS GHOSTS

The Religious Ghosts are adrift, unable to totally make the transition out of religion like the Abandoners, but equally incapable of making sense of religion in their lives. They remain tethered to a religious heritage, but never feel rooted or at home within it. One woman who is Jewish said, "I want to stay connected to my heritage and traditions. But I'm a liberated, professional woman. I go to Temple, but I'm not really there, because there's really no place for me in the Jewish religion."

This is the plight of the Religious Ghosts. They are there, but not there. Like Marcella, they will continue to show up until they decide that God has indeed said, "Go away." I am always astonished at the resilience and tenacity of these Religious Ghosts, for many cling to religion despite some serious religious abuse. Some are not aware that they are "Ghosts;" they drift in to church, drop the offering in the plate, and leave without making any real connection. Other Religious Ghosts know that they "aren't there." They just don't know how to make religion come alive for them in a healthy way.

I met Claire when I was serving as a Spiritual Advisor to a hospital treatment program where her fiance, Jim, was the Administrator.

Over the course of my monthly visits, Claire shared the history of her three-year ordeal with her first husband's church.

CLAIRE'S STORY

"Even though I've always gone to church, I was never very religious. I just sort of took it all with a grain of salt. When I met Bill, I knew he was active in a church, but I didn't really know much about it until after we got married," says Claire.

Slowly, Claire says, she and Bill both became involved with their small church and its charismatic leader, Pastor Smith. As time went on, she was so consumed by the duties of marriage, motherhood and church life that she did not notice how increasingly angry and irritable Bill had become. On a few occasions, Bill had hit and shoved her, but afterwards had been very contrite and ashamed. When Bill's physical assaults on her and his sexually inappropriate behavior around the children caused her to seek counseling from the pastor and elders, she expected that they would order him to get help.

"I should have known something was wrong when we went to couples counseling and it was like I was on trial for not being a good Christian wife," she says. "In other words, I wasn't supposed to complain, and certainly wasn't supposed to make it public." This was after Bill had been convicted of battery and she had begun divorce proceedings. "I don't know how they did it, but by the time they got through with me, I was so confused, I let him come back." And of course, he beat her again.

What followed was an horrific ordeal in which Claire was harassed and persecuted for first refusing to allow Bill back into the home, and then for filing complaints with the church administration over Pastor Smith's role in abetting further harm to her family. "Another family resigned from the church in protest of how I was being treated, but the church blamed me for this as well!" Claire resigned from the church, expecting her resignation to put an end to things. Yet they continued to harass her, demanding that she publicly forgive her ex-husband and Pastor Smith. They refused to accept or acknowledge her resignation in order to force her to admit she had been wrong. One of the letters they sent to her read,

Dear Claire,

It is with fear and trembling that I write this letter to you. I know you are aware of our meeting last Sunday night. I know this is true, because you were invited to it. It was because of our love for you that it was called. I believe there was not a person there that would not have, humanly speaking, wanted to do something else. I believe our love for you was exhibited in this meeting, as well.

Claire, we as a church, believe that you have left off following Christ. This is evident by certain sins. These sins are continuing separation from your mate without, as far as we can tell, any intent to reconcile; speaking reproachfully to others concerning him; an unwillingness to hear the call of the church to turn from these sins; and a continual negative relationship toward the church leadership.

Our call as a church is to exhort you to turn from these sins. To turn, we mean some outward evidence that you are dealing with them. If you do not, we will withdraw our fellowship from you on _____.

Claire, we do not stand above you. We are sinners just as you. It is just as possible for us to sin as you. We take this action by faith with the hope and prayer that the Lord Jesus Christ will use it in your life for good. Our door is open for reconciliation. If we can help you in dealing with these sins, please contact us. We will be praying for you.

In Christian love,
The Membership of the _____ *Church*

She received a barrage of similar letters from the church leadership, accusing her of sinfulness in her adamant pursuit of a divorce and her refusal to absolve the church leadership of complicity in the battery. Each letter totally discounted or ignored Bill's abusiveness and the probability that he had been sexually abusing his daughter, and perhaps his sons. Nothing was wrong with Bill; Claire was wrong for trying to leave him, and for telling people what was going on. Her pain was heightened by the fact that these people literally would not leave her alone. Even after she resigned from the church, she continued to receive harassing phone calls and letters. Not only did they refuse to help her, but they would not simply let her leave and begin her healing process. They were almost vicious in their determination to force her to publicly admit that refusing to forgive Bill and Pastor Smith was the only thing wrong with the marriage or her relationship with the church.

Not only did Claire not forgive them, she has not entirely forgiven God. Today, she has a very distant and guarded relationship with God. Trust is an issue, particularly with people in authority. This creates difficulties also in her new marriage to Jim. Claire also wrestles with the issue of God, religion, and their place in her life. "I want to be part of a church family," she says. "I miss that. It's part of what I grew up with, and to me, it should be part of my life and my marriage. But I'm afraid to get too involved. I don't want to get hurt again."

Claire remains estranged from God. In her mind, God is too closely allied with judgment and abuse. The message which came through loud and clear from her church was that God is not on her side, and as a result she feels confused and betrayed. She continues to seek a church in which she feels safe enough to allow herself to get involved.

Like most refugees from religion, the refugees in our stories have had a variety of experiences with religion. Some, like Claire, suffered outright abuse. Others, like David, brought their own issues with them into an unhealthy religious environment that magnified and reinforced those issues. Anna is the first to say that on the whole, her religious upbringing was "pretty mainstream," but that the people passing on what were then the standard messages about sex and sexuality had no idea of how those messages would affect a child who had been abused at such a young age. Yet within each of these stories can be found the common issues that send all the refugees from religion into spiritual exile.

What Are They Fleeing?

As we said earlier, people become religious refugees because some aspect of religion either does not make sense, or else it makes them feel unacceptable to God. Women in particular often have trouble with the patriarchal sexism of most religions. Many people flee the "one-way-only" rigidity, and the accompanying fear, shame and guilt when that one "right way" feels terribly wrong. Others are confused by the messages about "transcending" our mortal selves, or seeking the "higher" self, because these teachings offer no tools for dealing with those mortal, human feelings and traits and instead often trigger a war between the so-called "lower" and "higher" selves. And an increasing number of people are driven away, confused and angered by the traditional religious teachings about sex and sexuality. These are the aspects of unhealthy religion that disconnect people from their spirituality and alienate them from God.

"JUST WAIT 'TIL YOUR FATHER COMES HOME!"

I used to jokingly invite people to create an image of God the Daddy, to try to bring God closer. For many people, the image of "God as Father" has become a barrier to a healthy, adult relationship with God. As we saw in Chapter Two, God is vulnerable to our experiences or fantasies of "father." For me, God the Father was often confused with the father whose arrival I dreaded when my mother uttered those fateful words, "Just wait 'til your father gets home!" Especially in my home, where "Father" also applied to the stern priests who tolerated no infractions from raucous schoolboys.

For many people, "Daddy" calls up the same kinds of memories of abuse, abandonment, criticism—or perhaps total indulgence, caretaking and unrestrained giving. To children who have been abused by a parent, the image of an angry, judging parental God would certainly be consistent with their own experiences: God is every bit as angry, inconsistent and crazy as Dad or Mom. They grow up finding nothing wrong with such behavior, and indeed, never seem to question it in themselves or others. Other children, in the face of an abusive parent, may long for the gentle, loving God who is going to come and fix everything. One day. And when that day never comes, and the pain continues, the disappointment turns to rage which is either turned on God, or on themselves. Such people struggle and struggle to come to terms with understanding why God did not help them in their hour of need. Many of them become refugees from religion.

Let's look at some liturgy, prayers and hymns that are supposed to assure us of a loving, caring God, but which often have the opposite effect. Hidden within the teachings, rituals, doctrine and dogma are seeds of shame, guilt and helplessness, messages which create or perpetuate dependency on people or things outside ourselves. The result is an extremely passive relationship with God, in which God does things *for* or *to* us, but never *with* us. This child-like dependency creates unrealistic expectations of God and of ourselves, and of the relationship between us and God, and clashes with almost everything we are taught about being mature, responsible adults. It keeps us from being able to recognize where and how God is present in our lives. The resulting conflicts ultimately lead either to an abandonment of ourselves and our spiritual power, or of God.

In the Episcopal Eucharist, the Prayers of the People opens by beseeching God to hear our prayers. Then it asks that grace be bestowed on all the bishops and ministers *"that they may, by their life and their doctrine, set forth thy true and lively Word, and rightly and duly administer thy holy Sacraments."* Right away, it reminds us that the clergy are charged with setting down God's word. Then it goes on to say:

And to all people give thy heavenly grace . . . that with meek heart and due reverence they may hear and receive thy holy Word, truly serving thee in holiness and righteousness all the days of their life.

This is language of passivity, disempowerment, and a childish relationship. Not only is it a childish relationship, but an unhealthy one, for almost every verse contains the words "beseech . . . grant . . . give." This is a remote "gimme God"—a father whose children must beg and plead and perform for attention. There is no adult challenge, no call to active participation.

Earlier, we saw in the story of Bartimaeus the miracle of the active partnership we can create with God when we take action. Yet unfortunately, most of the liturgies for healing focus on magic, and in doing so, perpetuate passivity and dependency. In the prayer for Laying on of Hands and Anointing, God is asked to send the Holy Spirit to bless the oil so that the clergy doing the anointing can heal as the apostles did. The priest beseeches God to *"sustain you with his presence, drive away the sickness of body and spirit, to give you that victory of life, and peace which will enable you to serve him both now and forevermore."* God is being begged to drive away sickness so we can continue to serve. In this one section alone we find reinforced several disempowering messages:

1. The combination of oil and clergy is the magical cure.

2. God will take away sickness.

3. God wants us to be healthy so we can serve *him*.

It plants the subtle seeds of doubt: If we are sick, are we valuable to

God? Can we serve? If we are not healed, what does it mean? Was the oil not blessed properly? Were we not deserving of healing? Are we being punished for something else we did in the past? Has God abandoned us?

One hymn that traditionally has been used to offer comfort is "What a friend we have in Jesus:"

> What a friend we have in Jesus; all our sins and griefs to bear.
> What a privilege to carry everything to God in prayer.
> Oh, what peace we often forfeit, oh, what needless pain we bear.
> All because we would not carry everything to God in prayer.

Hymns like this have become the cement that bonds us in help-lessness, confusion, and in rage, when we carry things to God in prayer and the peace doesn't come, the pain doesn't end. And why is it a *privilege* to pray, especially to someone who is supposed to be a friend? For those who grow up singing these kinds of hymns, the subliminal message builds up over time: We are unworthy and helpless; we must beg, beseech, sup-plicate God to be in our lives. Is this an adult relationship? As adults, would we choose a friend whom we must constantly beg to help us? Only if we are extremely co-dependent and in need of therapy! Similarly, would we describe a parent-child relationship as healthy if the child is constantly forced to beg for parental love, nurture and care? This is exact-ly the kind of relationship which is often described as dysfunctional, because it emphasizes performance, duty, and above all, self-denial.

Attempting to provide alternatives to these kinds of hymns, some modern songwriters try to write more empowering hymns that are intended to abandon the shame and guilt and reinforce self-accep-tance. Yet even some of these are disempowering in their celebration of loving ourselves the way we are. The song "I Love Myself the Way I Am" has become very popular in my church, and when I first heard it, I thought it was a good song for nurturing self-love. Then I started noticing that some people were using it almost as a cop-out to avoid taking responsibility for themselves.

> I love myself the way I am;
> there's nothing I need to change.
> I'll always be the perfect me;
> there's nothing to rearrange.[3]

If that were true, I could still be drinking, abusing people with reli-gion and I wouldn't need to change, because I could love myself the way I was: arrogant, abusive, irresponsible and full of pain. Yes, I need to love and accept the old Leo who was in such pain, but that doesn't mean that my behavior and attitudes were acceptable. There was definitely a lot to rearrange in my thinking and way of life. Believing that you should be acceptable "just as you are" is a set-up for rejection and hurt. This is what happened to David: he didn't learn the difference between accepting that his feelings are valid, and dumping them on people. The "unconditional love" he thought he had found in his church apparently did not extend to inappropriate displays of anger. What is sad in David's case is that his experiences only reinforced his belief that he is unacceptable when he is being real.

What About God the Mommy?

Another limitation of the image of God as Father is that it creates a motherless family of God. I have heard children ask, "If God is our father, who is our mother?" Catholicism solved that one by elevating Mary to divine Motherhood, but it is a secondary role at best. The Holy Trinity is comprised of a Father, a Son, and a Holy Ghost or Holy Spirit that is usually referred to as He or Him. Mothers, daughters, sisters, wives and lovers are relegated to positions of servitude and that abusive attitude has been woven into our society, trapping both men and women in its tangled web in so many ways, both obvious and subtle. This male trinity reinforces the sexism, co-dependency, and general second-class position of women.

Like other single-father households in which the only females are servants, the family of God lacks the feminine influence which can offer balanced parental role models. This imbalance is what drives some of the refugees from religion to a matriarchal or feminine-based belief system. Matthew Fox in particular advocates a feminine-centered cosmology. His concepts of "original blessing" are an attempt to overthrow the oppressive yoke of sin, shame and patriarchal authoritarianism. Yet, despite the desire to create a gentler, more nurturing view of the universe, a matriarchal system still lacks balance. More important, whether you believe in God the Father or God the Mother, if you still cast yourself as a little child in your universe, you are likely to be ill-prepared to develop an adult relationship with Father-Mother-God.

"GOD WILL GET YOU"

I used to roar with laughter at the American TV show *Maude*, when the actress Bea Arthur fixed someone with her baleful glare and intoned, "God will get you." I often wonder if the writers of that show were consciously striking at the core of our religious psyche when they made "God will get you" one of Maude's running gag lines, or if they just had a sixth sense for getting laughs. Yet for many people, the belief that God will get them is no laughing matter. It keeps them in fear and flight from themselves, and from God. There are also those who are equally afraid God won't get them—won't take care of them, make it better. Or they are angry that God didn't get them—didn't take away the problems, heal the pain, answer the prayer the way we wanted it to be answered.

What kinds of things will God "get" us for, and why? In addition to those outlined in the Ten Commandments, when I was growing up I heard a seemingly endless procession of "Thou shalt nots," accompanied by a variety of dire threats:

- If you masturbate, you'll go blind.

- Don't show people your real feelings; people will think you are weak.

- Sex outside of marriage is a sin and damnable.

- Never argue with your parents, elders or superiors. Disobedience is a punishable sin.

- You should never criticize the *Bible*, religious teachings or the Church. Hell is filled with heretics.

- To please God, fill your life with prayers, meditations, retreats and rituals.

Perhaps, as I did, you learned early not to show your feelings. Maybe you, like Anna whom we met earlier, heard that if you have sex outside of marriage, you are not nice and will be ostracized. You might be like David who grew up expecting to be rejected and criticized if he made a mistake. Perhaps you, too, find yourself struggling with qualities about yourself you don't like, but don't realize have sprung from the religious teachings you have received in your childhood:

Denial   Co-dependency and caretaking
Magical thinking   Helplessness and powerlessness
Control/authoritarianism   Discrimination/sexism
Judgmentalness   Blaming/scapegoating
Victimization

Alongside these messages are a host of scriptures and liturgies that in many subtle ways reinforce the idea that God holds all the power in our lives, and we had better keep our noses clean if we want to receive God's gifts. Let's examine how the rituals and liturgies of the Episcopal Church reinforce these dysfunctional qualities. Although I'm using examples from my own religious denomination, the structure, inferences, and choice of words are virtually the same in most Catholic and Protestant services. And I think you can find similar kinds of messages in other religious and philosophical writings. Look at what is said during the marriage and christening services—two of the most widely heard and used services. The prayer following the marriage rites includes such lines as:

> *Give* them wisdom and devotion in the ordering of their common life . . . *Grant* that their wills may be so knit together in your will . . . *Give* them grace when they hurt each other, to recognize and acknowledge their fault, and to seek each other's forgiveness, and yours . . . *Bestow* upon them, *if you will, the gift and heritage of children* . . .

I'm sure you noticed the frequency of the plea to Give, Grant, and Bestow. No wonder so many people get childishly angry at God when things don't go right. Listening to this prayer, it doesn't sound like the Church is giving people credit for using God's gifts. God is being asked to grant wisdom and devotion, like the couple doesn't have the inner spiritual insight to recognize and want to publicly commit to each other's strengths.

These prayers reinforce the idea that children are gifts from God. In fact, the prayers said at a baptism reiterate this over and over: *"Since it has pleased God to bestow upon _____ the gift of a child, let us now give thanks . . . "* If you cannot conceive children, does this mean that God is displeased, and doesn't think you are worthy of the gift of children? How painful this must be to those who so desperately want children, or worse, have suffered the death of a child. This service also certainly fosters the notion that babies, being gifts from God, magically appear without any responsibility on our part. Even in adulthood, God is still like Santa Claus, bringing presents to those who are good. I would rather see prayers which affirm that sexuality and the depth of human love is a gift, and that the choice to create a child is a sign that we acknowledge and accept this great responsibility.

Then there is the confessional Prayer for the Reconciliation of a Penitent, which starts out, "Bless me Father, for I have sinned," and then goes downhill:

> Therefore, O Lord, from these and all other sins I now remember, I turn to you in sorrow and repentance. *Receive me again* into the arms of your mercy, and *restore* me to the blessed company of your faithful people . . .

I can see why people are afraid to risk making God mad. It's clear from this prayer that if you screw up, you're out! Notice how the penitent is required to ask to be received into God's arms again. I do not believe God gets so angry that we must beg to be received. I do think we can become so ashamed we would believe God would toss us out like parents issuing "tough love." I do not believe we must ask to be given wisdom; rather, I believe it is always within us. Sometimes, we forget we have it, or can't see how to use it; in those times, we need to be reminded, to affirm that wisdom is available to us. But I don't think God gives it to us in exchange for good behavior.

When we are co-creators with God, we know that we have permission to use our faculties—our minds, emotions and bodies. We no longer must fear retribution from an angry, wrathful God.

In *A Return to Love*, Marianne Williamson notes that a thought system based on fear is what separates us from God.[4] I have met so many people who live in fear—of being judged, of not having enough money, or a job, or being able to take care of themselves. They are often so paralyzed by fear, they cannot make decisions for themselves. They either totally rely on other people for everything, or refuse to accept any kind of assistance at all, even when they make the same mistakes again and again. These are the people who run through a variety of religions and belief systems, looking for a pathway to God's power, for a formula which will make them that "perfect channel."

"WE MUST RISE ABOVE OUR BASER INSTINCTS"

True spirituality is, ultimately, the essence of being real, of being honest with ourselves and others about our feelings and thoughts. What religion often does is teach people to abhor and deny their own reality. The reality of being human is that we are imperfect. We are vulnerable to illness, to mental or physical breakdown. Our emotions can keep us in turmoil. We are not spiritual puppets: we are free to choose between positive or destructive actions, and sometimes, innocent people pay the price for other people's choices. Religion is often presented as the antidote to our humanness—the way out of sickness and pain; the way to insure that we will all choose positive actions. In this view, spirituality is seen as the proof that we have risen above our humanness. So people believe that if they are in pain, if they are angry, or jealous, or feel inadequate, the very presence of those feelings means they are not spiritual. So they rush to "transcend" or somehow get rid of, those so-called bad feelings.

Ultimately, those feelings are not transcended, but merely repressed, thus creating the Shadow or dark side of human nature. I see people in churches, treatment centers, support groups, and therapy working diligently on removing these allegedly undesirable qualities. Outwardly, people project the image of what they are told is acceptable, not what is real. They are told not to show anger, told to "be brave" and not show pain, fear, or grief. They may be told not to "air the family linen" in public, so they become walled up and guarded. Perhaps they were told never to hurt people's feelings, so they become co-dependently dishonest. They may learn early on that making a mistake could result in physical or emotional abuse, ridicule or shame, so they become perfectionistic and controlling. They may be told that sex is dirty or base, so they bury their sexual feelings under food, religion, or work.

In the book, *Meeting The Shadow*, I found an excellent definition of our Shadow side and how we get it. Describing the fracturing of the self that happens when a child is criticized for having certain character traits, author Harville Hendrix writes that we split into three kinds of false or Shadow selves:

1. Your "lost self," those parts of your being that you had to repress because of the demands of society.

2. Your "false self," the facade that you erected in order to fill the void created by this repression and by a lack of adequate nurturing.

3. Your "disowned self," the negative parts of your false self that
   met with disapproval and were therefore denied.[5]

The real parts—anger, grief, pain, sexuality, honesty, courage—are
denied, shunted aside, where they often band together to become the
"Shadow" side. I meet so many people who are forever on guard
against their Shadow side popping up and causing trouble. Most of
these people don't recognize that unhealthy religious messages helped
create their Shadow sides; paradoxically, they try to use those same
unhealthy messages to remove the Shadow parts.

What needs to be understood is that we cannot remove these
aspects of our human nature. They are part of what makes us human.
Often in mythology, monsters or non-human beings are depicted as
having no shadow. Vampires can't be photographed or seen in a mirror—they cannot see themselves reflected back to them. Without these
parts of ourselves, we would be flat, one-dimensional. We would not
be real. We would have no way to reflect or mirror ourselves, to see
who we are. Yet the Shadow self is often what is stuffed into the God-
Box, where it can fester until it grows into the truly monstrous behaviors of which we humans are capable. But people *want* to be real, to
feel acceptable and loved. So they leave the place where they feel
unloved and unwanted to find a place of acceptance and belonging.

When you believe that God is either going to "get you" (or abandon you) for bad behavior, and reward you for good behavior, you stop
being free. You are no longer able to make spiritually free choices, and
instead have your choices dictated to you by fear. But like political
refugees, the refugees from religion simply want the freedom to be who
they are. They are seeking the freedom to doubt, to engage in dialogue,
to discover God in different places. Messages which restrict questioning and dialogue, which serve to isolate and exclude, rob people of the
freedom to really choose and develop their own relationship with God.
As Arthur Melville writes:

A person denied the opportunity to think or to believe as he or
she chooses, manipulated by fear of punishment, is not free.
Human beings prevented from developing their potential are not
free. God cannot be attained except by free choice, despite the
belief that the sacraments work their effects of themselves. The
overbearing parent who continuously controls the child steals
that child's most precious gift. The jailer who guards the prisoner

is also a prisoner. Being unable to speak to God in one's own way, from one's soul, is being unable to relate to the Creator with the most magnificent of divine gifts: creativity.[6]

RELIGION, GOD AND SEX

No single aspect of human creativity has been as damaged by religious intrusion as our human sexuality. It is one of our most precious gifts, and sadly, the one most abused in the name of God. I have rarely encountered anyone who did not have some fear, shame or confusion as a result of religious teachings about their sexuality.

When I was growing up, sex was a Big Secret. It was revealed in whispers, explored behind closed doors, sometimes fearfully, sometimes with smirks and the secret thrill of the forbidden. To talk about it was WRONG; to even think of "doing it" (assuming one knew what *it* was and how one did it) was a MORTAL SIN punishable by a variety of horrendous blights ranging from going blind to burning in everlasting hell.

In England, where I grew up, expressions such as "doing the dirty" are used to described the sex act. Long before I learned that it was OK to "do it" only after marriage, I learned via the schoolyard that I was the result of my parents having "done the dirty." Did that make them dirty? Did it make *me* dirty? So the loudest message I got about sex was that it was a dirty, shameful, secret thing. In the face of such a message, how then could I dare ask the questions, share the fear and confusion which are the natural companions of puberty? I couldn't, and that fear and confusion got locked up into the God-Box of shame I carried at the bottom of my being. This shame became the wellspring of my alcoholism and religious abuse.

As I mentioned earlier, I decided against joining the Jesuits because of their position on birth control. To be honest, the idea of celibacy did not appeal much to me, and not just because I didn't want to remain celibate. I had spent enough time amongst both Catholics and Protestants to know that the issue of priestly celibacy was a thorny issue. I had seen the double lives, the deceit and hypocrisy, the secret torment of men deprived of the most sacred of God's gifts. I knew monks who were told by their Abbots, "Don't get caught" having secret relationships with women, or amongst themselves. I saw priests become almost

vicious in their treatment of women as inferiors or would-be temptresses in order to stifle their physical and emotional responses. I did not
want that kind of service to God.

Both James Kavanaugh and Arthur Melville relate from their own
experience how Catholic priests are ill-prepared to talk to people about
sex. Even in the Church of England, where priests can marry, few are
trained to do more than spout scripture and doctrine. My friend Father
Ralph will tell you with absolute sincerity that he is extremely well-
versed in marriage counseling because he spent several years as the
Bishop's secretary, and as such, handled all the Bishop's correspon-
dence concerning sex and marriage. His rationale is that who better to
know what to tell people than the Bishop?

No wonder there is such rage amongst the refugees from religion.
As one man said to me, "Try explaining why premature ejaculation is
a marital problem to a guy who isn't even supposed to know how an
orgasm feels. I mean, to a priest, it's probably a good thing, but let *him*
explain that to my wife!" Such situations explain why religion does not
make sense to many people when the teachings about such basic
human functions are so distorted.

Up until probably the last ten years, clergy were taught that sexuality
is merely part of the moral base which it is their duty to oversee. Most were
not taught to counsel people on sexuality, except in the black-and-white,
dogmatic "wait-until-marriage-do-it-only-to-have-children-and-above-all-
don't-enjoy-it" terms. Nothing in my preparation for the priesthood
taught me anything about human sexuality and relationships. I learned
about those things during my treatment for alcoholism and later, in my
training as an alcoholism and eating disorders counselor. In fact, my
training for the priesthood did not include *any* training in the so-called
people skills. I was taught how to run the governmental and organizational arms of the church so that vestments were kept clean, flowers on
order, births, marriages, baptisms and funerals properly conducted and
the church's coffers kept full. The so-called pastoral counseling was simply an exercise in dictatorship. "Do this, go here, do that." I certainly
would not have known what to do had a parishioner come to talk to me
about the spiritual issues that result from sexual abuse, or worse, tried to
report a clergyman for sexual abuse. Nor was I trained how to counsel
anyone struggling with issues of sexual identity or homosexuality.

In the Name of God

An incredibly large number of refugees from religion come from the ranks of the sexually abused, and from gays. These two groups bear grievous spiritual wounds, for often they have been abused in the name of God. I receive many heartbreaking letters from people who were sexually abused by clergy or religious people. They write almost pleading for me to help them understand why God allowed it, and most of all, for help in learning to let God into their lives again. The abuse they received not only damaged their sexuality and self-esteem, but created an almost unbridgeable chasm between themselves and God.

One of the most poignant accounts I have read of the effects of sexual abuse by clergy is in the case of those abused by a Massachusetts priest. One of the priest's principal accusers, told *People* magazine: "It's kind of like being in a jungle when you're a kid. It's bad enough as it is without having your guide—a priest—turn on you in that jungle."[7] For those whose childhoods are already scarred by dysfunction at home, clergy sexual abuse adds to the sense that the world is not a safe or friendly place.

What makes it so spiritually disastrous is that at some level, survivors of religious sexual abuse believe that *God* is the one who turned on them. Years of being conditioned to see clergy as God's representatives make it almost impossible to separate God from the religious sexual perpetrator. Several survivors have said virtually the same thing: "If you can't trust God, who can you trust?" Certainly, they cannot trust their own judgment, especially those who were exploited in adulthood. Many believe they deserved the abuse. Religious teachings about sex, coupled with other messages about God's wrath and judgment, combine to convince survivors of sexual abuse that *they* are the bad ones, as Anna described earlier.

In the case of those who are sexually abused by clergy or church leaders, they are often driven out, ostracized and shunned if they speak out. One woman who was abused at age 13 by her female Sunday School teacher and sought help from the Sunday School Superintendent found herself being branded a lesbian and ostracized. "My best friend's mother publicly stated I was no longer welcome in her home and I wasn't to ever speak to her daughter again." This woman's letter is one of many I have received from people who were persecuted, driven out of their churches, for trying to tell the truth about clergy sexual abuse. The mythology about clergy being "pure as driven snow" is so entrenched that many people actually believe that it is *impossible* for a so-called "man of God" to seduce, or sexually harass a member of the congregation.

It is not surprising that many of the refugees from religion are gay—persecuted by religious teachings which preach that they are evil, frequently driven out of their biological and religious families. Gays and lesbians often desperately struggle to create healthy spirituality in the face of wholesale spiritual abuse. Some of the most difficult counseling I have had to do, as either a priest or a hospital consultant, is with gay patients who are at war with themselves, the world, and God. I have had gay patients actually laugh in my face when I talk about self-acceptance. "My mother tells me I'm evil. My minister told me I'm an abomination. My ancestors practically came on the Mayflower, but the illegal aliens next door get more protection from the government than I do. What the hell good does it do to accept myself when the rest of the world wants to get rid of me?" cried one anguished lesbian. "I'm supposed to have been made in God's image. If that's true, then why does God hate me?" asked an angry gay man.

When I work with gays and lesbians, I explain my own understanding and beliefs. I do not believe we can choose our sexual orientation, any more than we can choose what sex we are, or the color of our eyes, or our bone structure. I don't believe that homosexuality is a disease or a birth defect, any more than being short or left-handed is a defect. For my part, I am less concerned with *why* people are gay, than with the effect being gay has on their spirituality, on their relationship with themselves, with others, and with God. I am far more concerned with the dysfunctional attitudes and beliefs and behaviors they have developed in order to make themselves feel acceptable to God, or with the beliefs that keep them separated from God. For in these beliefs and attitudes can be found their common ground with other refugees from religion.

No matter what specific issues have sent them into spiritual exile, all of the refugees from religion merely want to like themselves, to have self-esteem. They think that God's love should automatically give them self-love. Yet the things they do to win God's love often drive them into fear and self-loathing. One woman wrote to me, "I learned early that I became acceptable when I became religious. To be religious meant being perfect, and that meant everybody around me had to be perfect, too, so I raised my children in what I now know was a religiously abusive home—rigid and unforgiving of mistakes. I became judgmental and critical. I never felt that God loved me—that there was anything special or precious in me for God to love."

This is how a spiritually dead religion leaves people confused and angry, alienated from God and from themselves. Many have turned their backs on religion, never to return. Others want to find a religious home that will let them discover and nourish the specialness within themselves, secure in the knowledge that God is always with them.

Calling The Refugees Home

I wish I could sound it out through all the land: "Come home, refugees. We need you." There is a marvelous story in the New Testament section of the Christian *Bible* about Jairus's daughter. This little girl was very ill, and they sent for Jesus to hurry and heal her. But Jesus was not particularly concerned. "She is asleep," he assured the anxious friends who tugged and pulled and begged him to get a move on. When he got there, they were weeping and wailing because the child had died. Her distraught parents berated Jesus for not coming sooner. "She is asleep," he said again, matter of factly. And though she had appeared to be dead for over a day, he went to the child and awakened her, telling her overjoyed and astounded family to give her something to eat. Jesus was always practical, even at his most Divine.

In this story, I find hope. I think of my own life, of the number of people who shook their heads saying, "Leo's finished. His ministry is dead. He'll die drunk." Maybe you, too, have been written off as hopeless. Maybe you have written *yourself* off as hopeless. "It's too late. I can't change. What's the point?"

The point is, few situations in life are actually hopeless. Yes, there are often terrible tragedies: illness, violence, death. Here in California where I now live, there are many examples of beginnings that come from endings—changes that arise after earthquakes and fires and riots. A father mourning his murdered child bands together with another grieving father to pass a law preventing repeat offenders from being released from jail. Yes, their daughters are dead, but they were not without hope that they could stimulate change.

Elsewhere in the country, a woman persists in seeing that justice is done for her son and others like him who were abused by Catholic priests. Go against a system that has ignored sexual abuse by its clergy for 2,000 years? Now there's a hopeless situation. Yet Jeanne Miller and others like her stood their ground, kept the issue before the public, and the Pope finally acknowledged that the Church "has a problem." Not perfect, but it's a start!

So it is for religion. Perhaps, like Jairus' daughter, religion is not dead, but sleeping. And this time, the healer is not Jesus, but the refugees themselves. Who better to know what is wrong and what is needed than those who have left, who have wandered and explored, even those who drift about, disconnected?

Recently, I asked Anna, "What if there was a button you could push and poof! all religion would be wiped out, gone, evaporated. Would you push it?" Without thinking twice, she said, "Absolutely." Then I asked her to think: No religions anywhere would mean that there would be no more art, music, theater or philosophies to be inspired by religion—and that includes all the great artistic and political rebels whose religious revolts instituted great changes. "Hmmm," said Anna. "Maybe I'd only wipe out *bad* religion."

The worst thing we can do to religion is to leave it to the religiously unhealthy. It stops the challenge, the dialogue with religious intolerance and abuse. We can rarely influence change and acceptance by leaving. Certainly, for many there are grievous wounds that cannot be healed within a religious setting. But the final healing may be a return to religion as Wounded Healers to help spiritualize and revitalize religion.

My challenge to the refugees is: *Don't give up on religion. It is not dead. It is merely sleeping. When it is awakened and fed the nourishment of the Spiritual Values, it can enrich and enlighten our understanding of how all of life fits together.*

One of the reasons I returned to a Sung Mass format in my Recovery Service is to demonstrate how the church can be revitalized. Blending both the traditional and modern, we seek to make the Mass a living parable for how people can come together and create community. Episcopalians, agnostics, fundamentalists, gays, blacks, Asians, the hopeless and the hopeful all join in a common meal enriched by Bach's requiems alongside Bette Midler's *Wind Beneath My Wings;* the *Bible* alongside the *Big Book of Alcoholics Anonymous.* Religion is not dead. It has been asleep, comatose. Help us wake it up.

To the Religious Gypsies, the challenge is to realize that spirituality is a personal challenge—something they can work on themselves. To discover a safe place means to be involved in creating one. It is a process, not an event, to discover a place that feels reasonably comfortable and open to change, then stay put long enough to try to activate the Spiritual Values in their lives and within their religious setting.

The Abandoners need to realize, as Anna saw, that religion has a vital place in the fabric of all our lives—in our music, art, politics, government.

Too many of the Abandoners remain focused on the negative and destructive aspects of religion. The first time we celebrated the Recovery Mass, there were some people who had been away for a while and did not know that we had changed the format. One person sat through the service glowering and making faces, sometimes obviously "checking out" when something triggered painful memories. Clearly, he was not yet ready to be back in a formal Mass setting. But sadly, he was so consumed by his own pain that he was not able to notice the changes. Perhaps one day, he will be able to return, and will have much to bring to us when he does.

The Religious Ghosts need to realize that healthy religion is not about containment, but about change. Just as Jesus did not attack people with healing, but healed those who risked "plugging in" to his healing power, Religious Ghosts must recognize that only by connecting, getting involved, making moves, will they find anything of substance within a church. I often hear people say, "I haven't been to church for years, but we send the kids to Sunday School, because we think they need to be exposed to some kind of religious education." How will they know if their children are being exposed to the same kinds of things that caused their parents to drift away? The Religious Ghosts need to understand that education about religion, spirituality and God is not the sole job of the churches. It is a partnership.

Believe it or not, I was a kind of Religious Ghost—a mere reflection of the doctrines, dogma and rituals of the Anglican Church. Without knowing it, I was passing on my own spiritual disconnection, and I'm sure I created a number of refugees from religion in the process. As I've described, my experiences were so limited and stunted, so totally shaped by the structure of the church, that I had very little spiritual substance at all. My challenge as a Wounded Healer is not only to work to create a safe place within my individual church, but to challenge the body of the Episcopal Church to change how it trains and educates clergy.

Coming home is not an easy process for the refugees. Most refugees are carrying a large load of baggage that limits their ability to change, to heal the spiritual wounds. Many will have to revise their understanding of the relationship between religion, God and spirituality. Others will have to examine core beliefs about God to understand why changing religious denominations did not help them create a new relationship with God.

If you recognize yourself in any of these refugee stories, keep in mind that becoming a refugee from religion may be the first step to reclaiming your spiritual power. Now it's time to discover the other moves that can take you from being a religious pawn to a powerful player in the God Game.

NOTES

1. "My religious experience has taught me . . . " Melville, Arthur. *With Eyes to See: A Journey From Religion to Spirituality.* (Walpole, NH: Stillpoint Publishing, 1992). p. 83.

2. "The philosopher Jean Houston divides human experience . . . " Houston, Jean. *The Search For the Beloved: Journeys in Mythology and Sacred Psychology.* (Los Angeles: Jeremy P. Tarcher, Inc. 1987). pp. 23-27.

3. "I love myself . . . " Josephs, Jai. "I Love Myself the Way I Am." (St. Mary, Kentucky: Living Love Publications). p. 52.

4. "In *A Return to Love* . . . " Williamson, Marianne. *A Return to Love.* (New York: HarperCollins, 1992). p. 18.

5. "1. Your "lost self . . . " Hendrix, Harville, "Creating The False Self." Abrams, Jeremiah and Zweig, Connie, eds. *Meeting the Shadow: The Hidden Power of the Dark Side of Human Nature.* (Los Angeles: Jeremy P. Tarcher, Inc., 1992). p. 51.

6. "A person denied the opportunity . . . " Melville, Arthur. *With Eyes to See: A Journey From Religion to Spirituality.* (Walpole, NH: Stillpoint Publishing, 1992). p. 272.

7. "It's kind of like being in a jungle . . . " "Sins of the Father" *People.* July 2, 1992. p. 33.

5

Discovering The God-Box

We really believed we were the one, true church, and
none of the others were real Christians the way we
were. There were so many rules in that church that
we never enjoyed life at all. I lived and breathed
church—I almost didn't have to function in the real
world. If I did the slightest thing wrong, I was made
to feel so guilty about it. All I wanted to do was to
serve the Lord, but one rule in our church was that
women couldn't do anything except take care of the
men and the children. When they were building the
church, I helped bring food and drinks to the men,
but that didn't feel like much compared to what the
men were doing. I never felt like anything I did was
good enough. I started feeling like I was going to go
crazy any minute, always trying to figure out what I
could do that would be worthwhile.

Mildred B.

FRUSTRATION. HELPLESSNESS. INADEQUACY. GUILT. DESPERATION. AS
Mildred B. discovered, these are the results when you box God into a
rigid, "one-way-only" set of beliefs and teachings. In describing her
church and the role she was allowed to play in it, she illustrates why so
many people end up feeling disempowered, disillusioned, and unable
to create a healthy relationship with God.

Any beliefs that limit or restrict where and how we can find God create a God-Box. When we think we can find God *only* in church, in liturgy, in ritual, or when we can see God *only* in rainbows, sunsets, and flowers, we begin to build a God-Box. If we rely on God as a Fixer/Rescuer, we diminish not only God, but ourselves, because we become spiritually dependent rather than spiritually empowered. When we look upon spiritual power as something God bestows after we reach a certain state, we create a God-Box. When we shut off emotions or feelings in order to be acceptable, we create a God-Box.

Describing his own struggles as a "refugee" from Catholicism, author-lecturer Earnie Larsen says in *Recovering Catholics: What To Do When Religion Comes Between You and God:*

> No concept, theology or word about God is wide enough to explain God. God cannot be put into a box. God resists any and all efforts to limit what God can or cannot do by constantly demonstrating (often in the most incredible ways) that God is bigger than we are![1]

Yet so often we are told what God is and what we must do in order to be in a relationship with God. As Larsen points out, this is how our religion often comes between us and God. It does this with myriad sets of messages and rules which, as we saw in Chapter Four, are often confusing or misleading. From these messages and rules come feelings such as shame, inadequacy, perfectionism or powerlessness. The combination of such rules and messages, along with the resulting feelings and attitudes, forms a barrier between us and God that stays with us even when we try to change religions, or leave religion altogether. I call this dysfunctional combination the God-Box.

What Is The God-Box?

The God-Box is the spiritual baggage many of us carry from one religion to another. It is built from the collection of confusing messages and unhealthy beliefs about spirituality, God, and religion that most of us have been exposed to since childhood. The God-Box is what keeps us from being able to come to a new understanding of spirituality, and of God, no matter how hard we try to change. It contains the things that suffocate religion and make it unhealthy. The God-Box generates rigidity and perfectionism, exclusivity and judgmentalism, religious co-dependency and helplessness, denial, and magical thinking. The God-Box stops creative change, personal empowerment, and the process of maturing spiritually to create an adult relationship with God.

BUILDING A GOD-BOX

We actually begin building our God-Box in childhood, from our earliest experiences, plus the messages and teachings we received as children within our homes, schools, and churches. If we grew up in an atmosphere that did not nurture the Spiritual Values of Truth, Love, Change, and Harmony, we are likely to carry our childhood concept of God with us throughout our lives. Over time, this childhood image of God collects a tangle of beliefs, experiences, attitudes, and feelings that get stuffed into what becomes our God-Box.

To get our God-Box, we start with our childhood concept of God. From this concept come our Core Beliefs, which usually have to do with God having all the power and people being inherently bad or powerless. These Core Beliefs create a lot of fear about our powerlessness, and what we must do to get God to grant us power. From the combination of Core Beliefs and fear come a host of Unhealthy Religious Messages. These messages in turn cause great shame and guilt. Now we have this great weight dragging behind us: our childhood concept of God is crusted over with the Core Beliefs, fear, Unhealthy Religious Messages, shame, and guilt. We begin to be pulled apart spiritually; the connection between our Body, Mind, and Emotions stretches thin and even snaps. Now we are truly broken; pieces of ourselves are scattered about.

Unhooked from the source of our spiritual power we fall prey to Religious Co-dependency, and like other co-dependents, we begin to develop patterns of passivity and control in response to the Unhealthy Religious Messages and Core Beliefs. We try to reconnect to God by becoming either very child-like and dependent on a "Fix-It" God, or else we become controlling, super-rigid perfectionists so that we can avoid punishment and feel safe. Whether we create a passive or controlling relationship with God, we must rely on rules, ritual, and magical thinking to sustain the relationship and help us follow all those Unhealthy Messages. But the rules, rituals, and magical thinking only produce more fear: what if they don't work, or we don't do them right?

This takes us back to the fear that comes from the Core Beliefs, and Our God-Box is complete.

This is a very simplified explanation, and it is *not* written in stone. Some of you will have other Core Beliefs besides the two I describe here: that we are born innately sinful and powerless, and that only God can absolve our sinfulness and grant us power. These are the most common, but they are not the only ones. We all have different Unhealthy Religious Messages, and most of us rarely fall into total passivity or total control. It's usually a blend of both, depending on the kind of messages we received. Some of us stuff the broken pieces of ourselves into the God-Box not knowing what else to do with them. Others leave their disowned parts outside the God-Box and try to run away from them. Some of us stuff our concept of God into the God-Box with us, others drag it around chained to the God-Box, wondering why it won't fall off so we can get a new concept. No matter how we put it together, or what is inside it, the God-Box keeps us from creating a healthy relationship with God and separates us from our spiritual power.

Let's take each step and explore how this process works. I will describe how my God-Box developed. Perhaps it will help you see how your own God-Box may have evolved. We do not build our God-Boxes overnight. Indeed, they are ongoing projects until we learn to recognize that we have them and can begin to reverse the process.

Start With Your Childhood Concept of God

As I described earlier, my childhood image of God was a mixture of the "Bogeyman God," and the distant "Passive God" who was rather like my father. As long as I behaved, as long as I was the Good Son, then the punishing Bogeyman God would be kept at bay. If I behaved and minded the Church's teachings I could keep the Passive God safely at a distance, appeased, so that, like my father, he would not be called on to punish me. Only recently have I come to recognize that as a child, I was being the Good Son not to nurture the spiritual value in "goodness," but rather, to avoid punishment.

So it is not a surprise that when I became a priest this core belief carried over into my priesthood. I taught people to live the spiritual life in order to avoid being sent to Hell, rather than to nurture and create a healthy relationship with God. My prejudice towards non-Christians and those who did not share my beliefs was based in part on my judgment of them as "false prophets" who might lead me or others astray and thus cause retribution from God. Tragically, for me, fear was the basis of my faith, and it formed the base, the foundation, of my own God-Box.

Core Beliefs About God

Each person's God-Box is unique, because we are all different. How it is put together and the ways in which it stands between us and God will vary. Yet there are common elements to every God-Box. When the Spiritual Values are not active in our belief system, no matter what religion, culture, or background we come from, there are two Core Beliefs about God that almost everyone carries in some form or another. These Core Beliefs emerge to form the base of our God-Box:

We are born inherently sinful or powerless.

Only God or the Universe has the power to fix or change us; nothing happens to us except through the will of God.

These are the roots of spiritual disempowerment. They are tangled in the bedrock of religious teachings. Their poisonous tentacles wind and twist around our concept of God, encasing and trapping it, so that it cannot grow and mature with us. These roots slowly strangle our relationship with God, disconnecting us from ourselves and our world, leaving us spiritually withering and dying. Many refugees from religion describe a sense of spiritual deadness or numbness. They can feel the slow suffocation, but don't know what's wrong.

When I first began to examine these Core Beliefs, I actually thought I had escaped them. Although my church was not the hellfire and brimstone type, I realize now that all the liturgies, rituals and doctrines, combined with my mother's steadfast belief in things happening according to God's will, left me feeling powerless and very rebellious against the idea that people were irrevocably born bad. I'd have looked you in the eye and sworn I didn't believe in Original Sin, certainly not the way the fundamentalist religions taught it. Yet my very rebelliousness against the idea indicates that, somewhere deep inside me, lurked the fear that I was indeed helpless, destined to become a powerless pawn in the God Game. This belief certainly surfaced in the depths of my alcoholic self-pity, when I felt helpless and unable to change. So even if you have not been taught these beliefs as I've worded them here, I think you will find, as I did, that they exist in some form at the core of your beliefs about God.

Fear: The product of dysfunctional Core Beliefs about God

When our Core Beliefs about God are unhealthy or dysfunctional, they usually produce a powerful fear. There is the fear of what can happen to us in this life, and there is the even greater fear of eternal damnation. One woman wrote to me: "That old fear creeps in, old messages—don't doubt, don't question. What if, for just looking into alternatives to spirituality, I will be condemned? ... Exactly what must I do to preserve my eternal life?" Oh, how I identified with this woman's letter!

These Core Beliefs put a literal "fear of God" into us, and this fear is the glue that holds our God-Box together. It creates the idea that life is a series of punishments or rewards from God. If we are "bad," if our Shadow self pops out to do mischief, God will get us and we will feel miserable, either in this life, for all eternity, or both. If we scrupulously struggle to be good, which means perfect, God will reward us and life will run smoothly. When our experiences in life seem to reinforce those Core Beliefs, so that we cannot overcome this fear of God, we have begun to build our God-Box in earnest.

Unhealthy Religious Messages

Unhealthy Religious Messages (URMs) have infested our religious and spiritual beliefs. I call them URMs because they rhyme with worms. The URMs worm their way into our lives, spoiling our experiences of religion and God. Although I label them "Unhealthy Religious Messages," they include many of the social teachings and lessons learned from our childhood experiences.

Some of these messages and rules are:

- God does (or will do) everything for me if I get myself out of the way.

- If something bad happens to me, I must have caused it or "called it to me."

- A woman's purpose in life is to obey her husband and take care of the children.

- It's egotistical and arrogant to take credit or pride in our achievements. (If something good happens, God did it.)

- Service, suffering, and sacrifice are essential ingredients of the religious life.

- It is selfish to grieve for the dead because God has called them home.

- We must transcend or rise above all earthly pleasures and cares in order to be spiritually enlightened.

There are hundreds of variations on these messages and rules. But these are among the most common that people list when we do this exercise in workshops. I find that, when we break them down, they come under three main themes or headings:

A Particular religion is the only path to a true spiritual relationship with God. Most of the messages about exclusivity, absolutism, as well as religious authoritarianism and abuse of power fall under this heading. These are all the messages that limit where and how we find God.

Spirituality is about transcending our physical, earthly desires and needs. Alongside this theme is the idea that we are spiritually empty until God fills us, as well as the messages about not grieving for those who have died. These messages all come from the Core Belief that we are sinful and powerless. They create the belief that God and the Kingdom of Heaven are separate and disconnected from our physical existence and the Universe. They are also the seed of many of the taboos against sex, sexuality, and human pleasure, as well as being the source of the inability to cope with the dark or shadow side of human nature. And they are often the source of the "God will get you" messages.

Service to God is the surest means of receiving God's grace. This concept unleashes the host of messages about self-sacrifice, the secondary role of women, and beliefs about service being the only true discipleship. It also forms the core of much of religious liturgy and doctrine. These messages are often the cause of religion degenerating into a mindless duty that bars the way to genuine experience. They also create the confusion between miracle and magic that so often accompanies the use of ritual and prayer. These messages lead to an unbalanced view of God's Grace as being sent down to us in response to a prayer, a ritual, a ceremony (magic), rather than emphasizing our co-operation, involvement and partnership with God (miracle.)

When people become refugees from religion, they are often trying to get away from these kinds of messages and rules. But as a result, new messages and rules frequently reflect the same Core Beliefs in powerlessness and punishment.

For instance, many people leave fundamentalist religions that emphasize the inherent sinfulness and "badness" of human beings. Some of them end up embracing the metaphysical or New Age beliefs that the Universe teaches us lessons. This seems like a more positive understanding. Yet I have heard so many people say, "The Universe was teaching me a lesson," in the same way they used to say, "God will get you." When the Core Belief is that God is going to somehow "get you," all the new rules and messages filter through that belief and keep you stuck in the same kind of relationship with God. This is what happened to Jane, whom we met in Chapter Two. Her belief that she must do penance for making people angry went with her from Catholicism to Zen Buddhism. Her relationship with God had not really changed, she'd just put it in a new container.

What happens next is the beginning of a vicious cycle. The URMs produce fear, which produces more dreadful URMs, which produce more fear as we try to live with these messages and rules that often make no sense, or cause us to start to disconnect from ourselves.

Now Add Guilt, Shame, and Disempowerment

My God-Box was born not only of my fear of that Bogeyman God, but of the fear of Not Being a Good Son, to both my mother and the Church. This fear both fueled and was fueled by such Unhealthy Religious Messages as:

- Good children don't upset their parents.

- The priest, as God's representative on earth, is always right.

- Don't question or doubt God's Word.

- A penitent life is the way to the Kingdom of God.

Well, these URMs were confusing. In my house, there were two different sets of God's Word: One Catholic and one Protestant. What was going to happen to my parents if they kept on arguing about religion? And which priests should I obey—the Catholic ones or the Anglican ones? Guilt, shame, and disempowerment began to loom large in my life. In my rebellious adolescent years when I sought refuge and superiority in the teachings of rigid Anglo-Catholicism, I truly thought that I had solved the dilemma of Being a Good Son by embracing a belief system that wouldn't totally displease either parent, yet, in a more passive-aggressive way, it tweaked both their noses.

Except for not accepting the Pope as God's representative on earth, Anglo-Catholics are in other respects more rigidly Catholic than most Roman Catholics in their observance of the rituals and dogma, and more devoutly Anglican than the staunchest Episcopalian.

I thought surely I could relieve my secret guilt and shame about Not Being a Good Son by plunging headlong into religious life. Yet I was always the rebel, the outsider, even when I was steeped most heavily in it. I loved Oscar Wilde's works nearly as much as I loved the *Bible*. Indeed, in my hangover haze on the morning of my ordination as a priest, I grabbed what I thought was my *Bible*, only to discover in the midst of the processional that I was clutching my treasured edition of Oscar Wilde. (Now some would say that was definitely a "sign from God" that I was meant to write about connecting spirituality to my responses to the secular world!) When I made this discovery, I immediately was overwhelmed with fear and panic. What if the Bishop saw? My mother would surely be mortified. Would it cancel my ordination if I was ordained without a *Bible*? Defying Shame, I retreated into my usual arrogance. "Ha!" I said to myself. "This just shows I'm special." But although I loved telling the story, I never could suppress some twinges of guilt and fear.

Shame and guilt drag us into the quicksand of disempowerment, for they keep us from learning to use the Spiritual Values in our lives. Shame tells us we are no good, and never will be. Shame stops us from seeing the changes we have made. When Shame rules our lives, we are never good enough. This is one of the hardest battles I had to wage in understanding my own childhood trauma. For the twin of "Not Being a Good Son" is named "Not Good Enough." Certainly as my alcoholism progressed, the grown Leo hid his head beneath the pillows, trying to escape the shouts of "Not good enough" that echoed through my guilty conscience. I felt I had failed everyone: my parents, my Bishop, my congregation, and my God. Sadly, it never occurred to me until later that, in believing myself to be not good enough, I was failing myself.

Disconnect the Body, Mind, and Emotions
Shame, guilt, and the URMs team up to widen the gulf between us and God. They eat away at our spiritual Response-Ability by making us disown, discard, or disconnect from some aspect of our humanness. Many of the messages I got at home, at school, and from religion, all

reinforced my need to be right and perfect. I wanted to be a Good Son, I did not want to be teased for stuttering, and I wanted to please my mentor priests. But in order to always be right, I became abusive. I learned to bully and shame people so that I would always win the debate, the argument, the point. And when I couldn't bear to see the hurt in someone's eyes, I learned to disconnect from my feelings, so that I would not have to feel ashamed. Finally, when the pain became too great to disconnect, there was alcohol and religion to take me away from myself. Even today it is very hard for me to admit that I have made a mistake. It's even harder to reveal my true feelings. Working on some of the chapters for this book, I said to my editor, "Well, they'll get to see Father Leo at his weakest." My editor, who knows me very well, reminded me: "No, Leo. They'll get to see you being *real*, so they'll actually see you at your spiritual strongest. You're modeling a powerful move!"

Religious Co-dependency: Passivity and Control

Co-dependency is about giving our power away. When we believe that God has all the power in our lives and we have none we have become religious co-dependents—including those who have left religion. The so-called "control addicts" who try to maintain power by controlling everybody and everything have actually given away their power by seeking to control what is not theirs to control. They miss the spiritual power inherent in self-responsibility, for trying to control others is often used as a means to control or escape our own feelings. In this way, religious co-dependents respond to the world as either victims or perpetrators, or both.

I became the controlling type. Where my salvation was concerned, I did not want to leave anything to chance. No passively sitting by and waiting for God to come along and rescue me. Remember, I had learned well in childhood that you have to get God's attention and keep it. For me, the way to do that was to immerse myself in the rituals, rules, and doctrine of the church. But instead of using them to connect with God they became a means of measuring my self-worth, by how well and often I did them. They were my means of "scoring points" with God.

Other people become spiritual pawns, passively and childishly waiting for God to do something. One of my favorite stories is the one about a man who is taking a stand against a ravaging flood. As his neighbors drive away, urging him to come along, he steadfastly refuses to go. "God will rescue me," he intones. When the streets flood, the police come by in a boat, offering to take him. "No," he insists. "I'm trusting in God." The waters continue to rise until he's perched on the tip top of his roof. A helicopter rescue team flies over and throws out a rope, but he refuses to take it. "God will take care of me," he cries, as the rushing waters sweep over him and drown him. When at last he stands before God, he cries, "Why didn't you come? I trusted in you!" God replies, "What do you mean, I didn't come? I sent you a car, a boat, and a helicopter. What more did you want?"

People who live as spiritual pawns cannot recognize how God is involved in their lives unless God sends a burning bush or some other glaring magical sign. Even then, like the man in the story, they usually miss it.

Reliance on Rules, Rituals, and Magical Thinking

At this point, our God-Box is nearly complete. Having lost our spiritual connectedness to our Body, Mind, and Emotions, we try to gain spiritual power through the use of rules, rituals and magical thinking. Unfortunately, when we become pawns of the things of religion, those tools which were meant to bring us closer to God actually create a barrier. They separate us from God when they create fear or shame. The prayer or chant which is designed to help open channels to God becomes a burdensome duty: Have we said it correctly? Did we say it the prescribed number of times? What will happen if we don't do it right? The rituals themselves lose meaning, and become something we can do without thinking. A service or meeting becomes a thing to be dreaded: Do we have the proper clothing? Will we be judged for some kind of lapse? What will happen if we don't go? God becomes someone to fear, an angry judge, so we grow more rigid, more righteous, in our desperate attempts to avoid being judged.

Remember the Diocesan missionary who told me, "God will take care of it if we get out of God's way?" That is an example of powerlessness and magical thinking. We become spectators, sitting on the sidelines of our lives, safely out of God's way, waiting for God to score a touchdown for us. Our only involvement is to cheer God on.

And when it appears that God might not respond, there is yet more fear, and a frenzied bargaining with God. "If you'll just help me this time, I'll go to church all the time . . . tithe . . . give up smoking, drinking, overeating, sex. . . . " The control addicts grow more controlling. The passive co-dependents stay stuck in helpless victimization. At the end of my alcoholism and religious addiction, I had many rules and rituals for myself which I violated almost daily. At the same time, I grew more rigid with the members of my congregation. "Get the damn flowers onto the altar properly. Make sure the vestments are cleaned and returned on time. Keep those altar boys in line. Tithing has dropped off. Start a drive to increase it." And to be sure I got the message across, I made sure that the liturgies, the scriptures reflected the need to please God by keeping His House in order. If I kept all these things going, I wouldn't lose my job. I'd be OK. I had totally moved out of the Kingdom of God within me, and instead placed myself as ruler of my own kingdom, sadly believing this would please God, that God would then overlook my lapses. My God-Box was complete. It was now standing between me and God.

Now that we've looked at the components that make up the God-Box, let's see what goes inside it. First of all, there is more fear. The Core Beliefs produce fear. The URMs produce fear. Our religious co-dependency creates more fear. The more we struggle to create a new relationship with God and find that we cannot, the more fearful we become. Fear rules the world of religious co-dependents. I see so many people locked in fear, unable to take risks. What if they're wrong? What if they fail? Fear permeates their lives. Some become rigid, controlling perfectionists who live by rules in order to feel safe. The only way they can be sure they won't be used and abused is to be in charge of the world. The only way not to feel judged is to judge others. They are afraid to be different, thus fear anyone else who is different. The dogmatic, black-and-white mindset of the religious fundamentalist is born of this fear.

From the fear comes rage: at ourselves, at other religions, at the world, and even at God, because we feel disconnected and afraid when we are trying so hard to connect with, and feel close to, God. So many of the refugees from religion are in a fury because the promises they thought religion had made to them have not materialized. I have seen people doing anger work in treatment programs, pounding away at a pillow with a plastic bat, screaming at God, "I did everything You told me to. I went to church. I gave my tithe. I don't lie or cheat. I saved myself until marriage. I'm good to my parents. *Why am I not happy? Where are you?*" Other refugees, like Anna, are furious at the abuses and inconsistencies. Anna says that sometimes she is more angry at her religious upbringing than at her sexual abusers because it was religion that made her hate herself by telling her she was "dirty" and that she was at fault for being sexually abused.

Because fear and rage are often seen as "unspiritual," they are kept stuffed in the God-Box where they breed a host of beliefs and attitudes: judgmentalism, religious righteousness and absolutism, exclusivity and dogmatism, obsession with rules and being right, are all offspring of fear and rage.

Sadly, elements of the Spiritual Values get stuffed into the God-Box, too. If you believe there is only one path to God, you miss out on opportunities for choices. If you feel like a victim, a pawn of God, you sit and wait for people to rescue you or do things for you, so you never discover the spiritual power of action. You never get to make your moves with God, waiting instead for God to always make the move for you. If your belief system is rigid and excluding, you cannot discover Harmony within yourself, nor real Love. If you believe you must hide your feelings in order to be acceptable to other people and to God, the Spiritual Value of Truth is missing from your life. You do not know how to be real to yourself or anyone else. Often, the real you gets locked up into your God-Box.

Sexuality often ends up in the God-Box. So many of the URMs are about sex and sexual taboos, and they make no sense in the context of human emotions and experience. The confusion and conflicts caused by these unhealthy messages often cause people to leave religion, or to break apart spiritually. Alongside sexuality, comes sexism, sexual harassment, and even sexual addiction and abuse. They are often directly traceable to the Unhealthy Religious Messages about sex and the role of women.

Lastly, there is the Shadow self—those aspects of ourselves that we are told are not acceptable, yet which persist despite all our rituals, prayers, and meditations. When we are taught that some part of ourselves is unacceptable, we will often try to change or discard it in order to be accepted. Many of the unhealthy messages cause people to abandon important parts of themselves. Most commonly people reject feelings, particularly anger and sexuality. These parts of ourselves have frequently been labeled the Dark or Shadow side of human beings. Many religions try to explain the existence of calamity and pain as the work of some kind of dark, evil, or negative force. Religions, especially Christianity, pit the so-called good or light sides of humanity against the dark forces. Christianity in particular teaches us to try to remove or avoid these supposedly bad feelings, thoughts, or behaviors. Many of us are taught that these aspects of ourselves are signs of the Devil at work in our lives and we must get rid of them if we are to be granted Salvation.

How The God-Box Disempowers Us

The God-Box disempowers us in so many different ways. It breaks the spiritual connection between Body, Mind and Emotions, setting us at war against ourselves. It focuses us on God "Out There" so that we rarely get to discover God Within. By keeping us from creating a relationship with God Within, it distorts the Spiritual Values, which then takes us farther away from our spiritual power. It replaces the spiritually powerful moves of the God Game with a series of rules, empty rituals, and magical thinking.

THE DISEMPOWERMENT OF FEAR

Let's go back and look at the elements of the God-Box, to see how they create disempowerment. Our childhood concept of God, and the Core Beliefs about God that we begin with, are disempowering. Yet many people do overcome them. It is the element of fear that stops people cold, and begins the descent into true disempowerment.

Living in fear—of God, of people, places and things we are told are sinful or bad—deprives us from appreciating the gift of variety God has given us. In turn, that stops us from truly using all the resources available to us today to effectively create changes. It stops us from making choices, for we fear making mistakes. Living in fear of making mistakes or being wrong keeps us from knowing our own Truth and being real.

Fear of making mistakes is one of the most common disempowering aspects of the God-Box. It makes us victims and causes us to victimize others. If we expect to be punished for making a mistake, then we become perfectionistic and controlling. If we dare not admit to a mistake, then we frequently must find a scapegoat to blame for whatever has occurred. This becomes a double victimization, for not only is the scapegoat unjustly blamed, but we remain trapped in the mistake, rather than being able to correct it. The fear, guilt, and rage which often accompany this victimization add to the baggage that gets stuffed into the God-Box.

Fear leads to righteousness, exclusivity, and absolutism. These are all fueled by the "one-way only" messages that tell us "Follow these rules, these teachings, and you will be OK." "Don't question authority; others know better than you." There is a certain safety in righteousness, not to mention satisfaction. The word carries a host of attributes: goodness, virtue, rightness, blamelessness, nobility, elevation. Certainly we can aspire to attain these attributes, but how, and at what price?

People who feel wrong inside themselves often have a great need to outwardly look right. Those who are uncertain and indecisive, who do not trust their own instincts, frequently take comfort in the "rightness" of doing what they are told God or some other authority wants. There is no choice involved, no personal responsibility. I can think of no better examples than the ordinary, probably good-hearted citizens of Germany who were seduced by Hitler's "final solution" and ultimately became accomplices in the Holocaust. This is where that kind of mindless "rightness" can lead: to destruction and waste of human life and potential. But this is an extreme. There are more everyday forms of this absolutism and devotion to duty.

Johanna is a social worker who appears extremely conscientious and scrupulous about the ethical standards of her profession. The truth is, she does not trust her own judgment. Fearing failure and subsequent punishment, she perfectionistically does everything to the letter in order to feel safe. Checking on one of her clients, she had a feeling one of the children was being abused. Because the evidence she had did not meet any of the criteria for reporting to the authorities, she rationalized that it was not "correct" to include her "gut" feelings in her evaluation. In reality, she feared being discounted or put down. When the child was later nearly beaten to death, she was reprimanded for not having reported her suspicions and subsequently lost her job—the things she most feared and tried to avoid by rigidly following the rules. Her instincts were right, but she could not let herself trust them.

This kind of choiceless, mindless duty to form, to rules, is literally soul-murdering. Renowned child psychologist Alice Miller wrote *For Your Own Good* in an attempt to understand how the Holocaust could have happened. What she discovered was a system of child-rearing which, over generations, conditioned the German people to take *pride* in not questioning, in burying their own feelings and accepting parental wishes as their own. For generations of Germans, then, self-empowerment—the ability to think, to evaluate information and situations, and then act on their decisions—was slowly eroded. Thus, when Himmler spoke proudly of having exterminated the Jews, and compared it to killing off a life-threatening virus which could have wiped out the nation, no one questioned.[2] A great deal of human ingenuity and creativity was channeled towards this horrific destruction of life. If healthy spirituality allows us to be positive and creative, then this kind of negative, destructive use of human creativity is an example of unhealthy spirituality.

When we blindly follow rules in order to feel right, we lose touch with our spiritual "Response-Ability." Johanna's scrupulosity—that mindless adherence to rules—disconnected her from her feelings and instincts. Using only her mind, her intellectual "textbook" assessment, without the support of her body and emotions—the source of that "gut" feeling—damaged her ability to respond fully. Being unable to respond fully limited her ability to choose. When rules replace guidelines, when form overrides substance, we become pawns, at the mercy of somebody else's rules. Alice Miller observes that values themselves become unimportant, since it is obedience which is the goal, not the standards and precepts.[3] And with that blind obedience, comes more fear and rigidity.

Fear often combines with guilt to produce much of the rage that is carried in the God-Box. In *Childhood and Society*, Erik Erikson explores what happens to choice and responsibility when initiative is repressed by fear and guilt. When children begin to take initiative, he says, there is a danger that parents may overreact and stifle that curiosity. The result in adulthood, he says, is a "powerhouse of rage" which must be submerged as hopes and dreams are repressed.

> The resulting self-righteousness—often the principal reward for goodness—can later be most intolerantly turned against others in the form of persistent moralistic surveillance, so that the prohibition rather than the guidance of initiative becomes the dominant endeavor. On the other hand, even moral man's initiative is apt to burst the boundaries of self-restriction, permitting him to do to others in his own or other lands, what he would neither do nor tolerate being done in his own home.[4]

This is the source of much of the abusiveness the refugees from religion abhor. In David's story in Chapter Four, we saw that David is very quick to tell others the "truth" about themselves, believing himself to be of superior insight. But he does not accord others the same right he demands for himself; he will not let others share their observances and insights into him.

David's God-Box is infested with exclusivity. In order to feel safe and right, he has developed a need to be exclusive, superior, above everyone. But exclusivity cuts us off from nearly all the Spiritual Values. If we are exclusive, it means we are excluding someone or something. What does that really mean? It means we shut out so many things which contribute to our spiritual growth; we never have to examine our attitudes or behavior; we never have to change; we never get to see abuse, feel pain, discover God in our own human specialness; we never enjoy the rich varieties and diversities God created for our use and pleasure.

In a workshop I did on healing the wounds of religious abuse, a gentleman asked me about my "stand" on other religious teachers such as Buddha and Mohammed. As I talked with him, it became clear he had never read any religious or philosophical texts other than the *Bible*. I asked him if he ever ate Mexican or Italian or Chinese food. "Well, sure," he said. Did he find those foods satisfying and nourishing? "Certainly." Had it ever occurred to him that other religious teachers might offer a similar kind of spiritual sustenance? "No," he admitted ruefully, understanding my point about variety and difference. And this man was a minister!

Exclusivity uses fear, rules, dogma, and perfectionism as barriers to separate people from God. They create a false sense of self-worth based on how perfectly the rules are followed, the dogma upheld. Huddled behind the walls of exclusivity it is easy to justify shunning those who are different, to condemn whomever does not conform to the rules. During one of my appearances on the KABC Los Angeles "Religion On the Line" radio program shortly after the January 1994 earthquake, a caller self-righteously expressed the opinion that God had "sent the earthquake to punish the homosexuals in Hollywood." That statement was so shocking I could only reply flippantly, "If that's so, then how do you explain why God missed?" Needless to say, the caller abruptly hung up, probably more offended by my suggestion that God might have missed than by my challenge to the caller's religious judgmentalness. (For those unfamiliar with that earthquake, it struck north of

Hollywood, and to my knowledge, none of those who perished in the quake were gay. Thus my caustic "God missed . . . " retort.)

Exclusivity shuts God out, for if we are afraid to share our true selves, then we will never totally discover the spiritual power of God Within ourselves. In this way, exclusivity limits how and where we find God. It gives us only a few moves in the God Game. Many valuable spiritual tools lie in different denominations and faiths, new paths which can take us to a deeper understanding of God and Empowerment. When we can only find God in church, we never discover God in cultural diversity, in education, in science, art, and therapy. When we believe there is only one right way to worship or elevate spiritual consciousness, we close the door to many wonderful paths to God.

Exclusivity breeds another kind of false sense of self, the kind which says "I'm saved. I'm redeemed. I don't need any help except what comes from scripture" or else, "I can't change my nature. This is who I am and I'll just have to live with it." I see this in people whose sense of self has been grievously distorted by shame. This is sometimes jokingly referred to by therapists or members of recovery groups as being "terminally unique," but it isn't funny. People who think that they are the only ones with their particular problems live in fear of exposure. They also feel powerless to change. People who think that because they are religious, they don't need the spirituality of secular programs, cut themselves off from help, as do those who believe they either don't need help, or don't deserve it. This kind of exclusivity is spiritually deadly, for it cuts the connections to true empowerment. It is often born of denial: of self, of reality and ultimately, of God.

THE DISEMPOWERMENT OF
RELIGIOUS CO-DEPENDENCY

I often wonder if there would be any such thing as co-dependency if we did not have religious messages that teach us we are powerless and must look outside ourselves for power. I have noticed that people who have done a lot of work on their co-dependency issues are the ones who are more able to claim their spiritual power. This is because co-dependency recovery requires that we get in touch with our feelings, with our minds, with our bodies, in order to create a healthy relationship with ourselves.

There are many definitions of co-dependency, all of which involve powerlessness and a subsequent need to control everything so as not to feel powerless. Co-dependents generally fall into two categories. Some co-dependents control by trying to run everyone and everything according to their own system. But by far the largest group is comprised of those who control by giving up their power and responsibility to others. These are the so-called "classic" co-dependents who control by making other people responsible for what happens in their lives, good and bad. Describing this form of co-dependency, Earnie Larsen writes:

> All negative co-dependent imprinting is an assault upon the formation of a healthy being. All co-dependency is about the loss of identity and independence. It is also about the giving up of our power to decide appropriately, thus giving others the right to decide where we are good enough or not, right or not, acceptable or not.[5]

Yet religions often teach us that it is our spiritual duty to give our power to God. No matter what the belief system, depending on a "fix-it" God nearly always results in helplessness and powerlessness, and a host of co-dependency problems which afflict nearly all areas of life. We become hooked on magic, expecting God to do it for us, and missing the miracle which comes in discovering we have the power to create for ourselves. Religious co-dependents often live in terror of being abandoned or punished by God. Fundamentalists touch the TV screen, expecting to be healed; Roman Catholics go to Mass to earn rewards and say the rosary to receive blessings; people in Twelve-Step recovery groups soberly "hand over" their lives to God and in some cases wait (not always serenely) for God to make life easier.

These are all symptoms of a passive, childish relationship with God that is based on obedience, conformity, and service. Mildred, whom I quoted at the beginning of the chapter, wrote in her letter, "my husband left me because of my child-like dependence on God. I got sick and stopped paying the bills. I never worried about it, because I *knew* God would take care of it. The thing is, I just transferred this on to my husband and he didn't want to be God." Nor did he want all those bills! When God didn't keep the bill collectors away, she childishly expected her husband to deal with it, like a father who pays for a window broken by his son's errant baseball. Her belief that her husband was supposed to protect her was a direct by-product of the religious teachings which told her to be obedient and submissive—in other words, child-like. So she had a child's skewed sense of outrage at her husband's reaction to having his credit ruined—rather like the child who wails, "It wasn't my fault! Tommy didn't catch the ball!" when told allowances are going to be withheld to pay for that broken window. When God or the universe doesn't fix things according to our wants, we either tantrum and sulk like children, or emotionally beat ourselves unmercifully for not having been "good enough" to get what we wanted.

As Mildred learned, believing that God will fix us or solve our difficulties without much involvement on our part, can cause us great emotional pain. This belief has leaked out of religion and saturated many areas of our lives—psychology, Twelve-Step recovery groups, and secular literature. It is evident in the popular piece, "Footprints in The Sand," which is often used to illustrate the idea that God will or should pick us up and carry us through hard times.

> There was a man who had a dream in which he reviewed the footsteps he had taken in his life.
>
> He looked down and noticed that all over the mountains and difficult places he had traveled there was one set of footprints; but over the plains and down the hills there were two sets of footprints, as if someone had walked by his side.
>
> He turned to Christ and said, "There is something I don't understand. Why is it that down the hills and over the smooth and easy places You have walked by my side; but, here over the rough and difficult places I have walked alone, for I see in those areas there are only one set of footprints."
>
> Christ turned to the man and said, "It was while your life was easy that I walked along your side, but here where the walking was hard and the paths were difficult, was the time you needed me most and there is where I carried you."

The subliminal message inherent in such writings is that, if God doesn't pick you up and carry you, it's because you didn't deserve it, or didn't have enough faith, or lacked some essential ingredient. So many victims of any kind of abuse, especially if it occurred in childhood, believe the abuse happened because there was something wrong with them, or that they somehow deserved it. I have worked with a number of people who ask, bewildered, "But why would someone do that if I wasn't asking for it?" They truly feel they somehow deserved the abuse, because God didn't "pick them up." Tragically, messages about God rescuing us as in the "Footprints" piece torture people already badly wounded, as they wait, hope, pray, for God to stop the abuse.

I am perpetually astonished at how many of the homes and offices I visit have the "Footprints" verse prominently displayed. I am less surprised when people who use it as a standard of faith continue to stay stuck with their old religious baggage, feeling powerless and at the mercy of a God whom they believe is solely responsible for carrying them through crisis after crisis. Sadly, I have watched people slide into deep depression or relapse, waiting for God to come and rescue them. They are never able to see their own responsibility (ability to respond) for their situation, never able to discover the spiritual moves that lead them out of their predicaments. If God doesn't fix it, then there must be some lesson God wanted them to learn—something they need to do or experience in order for God to carry them through the next ordeal.

Yet the spiritually powerful message inherent in the "Footsteps" piece is the knowledge that God's presence is *always* within us. Personally, I don't think God carries me. Rather, I carry God within me. Sometimes, I forget that God is there; old messages and beliefs blind me, put up barriers, so that I forget to involve God in my actions. But God does not bail out in those times. Mostly, I think that our own beliefs prevent us from seeing how God is involved in our lives and sadly, unhealthy religious messages are often the source of these beliefs. This is a source of human passivity—that childlike dependence on God which makes people almost spectators of God's activity in the world.

When we are spectators of life and God's involvement in it, the rituals of worship, especially in this age of televangelism, become just another form of cinema. We watch, but do not participate. One man wrote, "I loved the *drama*—the *form* of the service. I didn't care if it was in Latin or English, or even what the words said, as long as it was performed perfectly." For him, it was more important for the sermon to begin and end on time, the music and rituals performed perfectly and dramatically, than for it to contain something which sparked a reaction—a dialogue with God. This is what I mean by not participating, by merely being a spectator. There are many things which we watch—art, ballet, theater, sports—which inspire in us appreciation of human creativity, and in that appreciation, we can involve God.

Experiences in our families may have told us to trust no one; but at the same time, we are told to trust God and the priest or minister implicitly. We are told to grow up and take responsibility, but religious messages tell us we are children of God and we must wait for God to direct our lives. Such conflicts lead to great confusion and anger, from which grows so much of what is understood as co-dependent behavior.

We sit and wait for God to use us, feeling insignificant in the scheme of God's world, like Mildred described at the beginning of the chapter. When we go through life feeling like one of God's pawns, we never get to know God as our Co-Creator and Partner. Feeling like pawns, we don't get to know that we make a difference, simply by being ourselves. One single human being can make all the difference in the world. I believe this is one of the messages to be discovered in the life of Jesus — to show the many ways we affect each others' lives. I think this is what Jesus meant when he said, "I am the way . . . " He was suggesting a way to live which nourished and enhanced how we treat ourselves and each other. Many people find a similar message in the movie, *It's A Wonderful Life*, in which Jimmy Stewart's character believes he's a failure until he is shown what the lives of people around him would be like had he not been there. What director Frank Capra shows us in that film is the spiritual power of accepting our own Truth—the reality and specialness of who we are and how important our connections are in the world. When we believe we are failures, worthless, base, unimportant, we miss so much of the transforming qualities of spirituality. In trying to transcend our own humanity, we not only miss the opportunity to transform ourselves, but the world around us loses our transforming presence.

TRANSCENDING OUR HUMANNESS

Some of the most disempowering elements of the God-Box come from the teachings and beliefs about transcending our humanness in order to "become spiritual." For the price of acceptance of these beliefs is that we must give up or disown parts of ourselves we are told interfere with the quality of our service to God. Yet the duties and requirements of that "service to God" are often what drive people out of religion, because serving God seems to always lead to feelings of inadequacy, powerlessness and self-hate. These refugees want to find a new way to serve God which permits some sense of dignity and self-worth, but they arrive at a new religion or belief system dragging the same old dysfunctional messages in their God-Box.

The most dangerous aspect of the messages about transcending our humanness is the shattering of the Body-Mind-Emotions connection. This is a necessary result of trying to get away from ourselves. But in trying to escape our physical, mental, or emotional selves, we are breaking apart the spiritual model that I believe is the key to self-empowerment. Immediately, we are plunged into a black-and-white/good-bad/light-dark world that divides us, pits the two sides against each other. In an excellent analysis of Robert Louis Stevenson's story of Dr. Jekyll and Mr. Hyde, author John Sanford observes that Dr. Jekyll was basically a good man of many fine qualities who recognized in himself some attributes which he believed were "bad." The personality of "Mr. Hyde" was created to explain and, more important, to ventilate, those supposedly "bad" parts of Dr. Jekyll. According to Sanford, Dr. Jekyll's inability to stop turning into Mr. Hyde came from the desire to get rid of all those parts of himself which Mr. Hyde embodied. Sanford notes that, had Dr. Jekyll been able to accept those parts of himself, he would have become a whole person rather than splitting into two.[6]

The story of Jekyll and Hyde is probably one of the best illustrations of what happens when we try to deny our "dark sides." We break apart. Yes, we may succeed in covering up this so-called shadow self, but the price is spiritual amputation, for when we disown a part of ourselves, we abandon or deny other spiritual aspects like dignity, choice, responsibility, and freedom. Trust, intimacy, sexuality, and safety in God also get discarded along the way. We cannot be whole, we cannot be real. The Spiritual Values of Love—embodying self-acceptance, Truth—being REAL, Change, and Harmony are all lost to us when we declare war on our own human nature.

This is especially prevalent in those who have been abused by religious leaders—clergy or church officials. One woman who called my office kept insisting, "But I was an adult. I consented. So there must have been something wrong with me that I didn't say no." This sense of being lacking or bad is also what is preyed upon by clergy or religious fanatics who claim to be "curing" some sin or defect.

The Core Belief that tells us we were created "in sin"—somehow bad, base or powerless—creates the Shadow parts. In *Meeting the Shadow: The Hidden Power of the Dark Side of Human Nature*, editors Zweig and Abrams write:

The human body has lived for two thousand years in the shadow of Western culture. Its animal impulses, sexual passions, and decaying nature were banished to the darkness and filled with taboo by a priesthood that valued only the higher realms of spirit, mind and rational thought. With the advent of the scientific age, the body was confirmed to be a mere sack of chemicals, a machine without a soul.

The result? The mind/body split became entrenched . . . Like a river bed, the split runs deep in our cultural terrain, creating polarities anywhere it touches: flesh/spirit, sinful/innocent, animal/godlike, selfish/altruistic.

We feel the terrible results of this paradigm—body as shadow—in our own lives as guilt and shame about bodily functions, a lack of spontaneity in our movements and sensations, and a chronic struggle with psychosomatic disease. The disowned body also appears starkly in today's dreadful epidemics of child abuse, sex addiction, substance abuse and eating disorders.[7]

Unhealthy religion creates the polarities Zweig and Abrams describe, and since these extremes have no middle, balancing them is difficult. Instead of bending, these extremes snap and fracture into pieces. The "bad" pieces—the fragments of our shattered spirits—go into the God-Box. The refugees from religion struggle to become spiritually whole without retrieving those broken pieces, and so end up feeling more incomplete than ever.

The God-Box, then, is the answer to the question, "Why can't I get it?" Most people don't know they have a God-Box. Few people realize that their childhood beliefs about God have not changed, or the extent to which that concept has shaped their lives. Perhaps, as you have read this chapter, you have been thinking about your own God-Box—how it evolved, and the effect it has had on your own relationship with God, and your ability to create healthy spirituality and claim spiritual power.

I hope it is helpful for you to understand that there is nothing inherently wrong with you, that it's not hopeless, you have the spiritual power to change. You just have this God-Box stuck to you, but you're going to learn how to take it apart and reclaim your power. You will discover a new freedom—the freedom to be yourself and accept yourself, the freedom to make your moves in the God Game.

NOTES

1. "No concept, theology . . . " Larsen, Earnie and Prague, Jane. *Recovering Catholics: What To Do When Religion Comes Between You and God.* (San Francisco: HarperCollins, 1992). pp. 28-29.

2. "Thus, when Himmler spoke proudly . . . " Miller, Alice. *For Your Own Good* (New York: The Noonday Press, 1990). pp. 79-82.

3. "Alice Miller observes that values . . . " Miller, Alice. *For Your Own Good* (New York: The Noonday Press, 1990). pp. 83.

4. "The resulting self-righteousness . . . " Erikson, Erik. *Childhood and Society* (New York: W.W. Norton, 1964). pp. 257-258.

5. "All negative co-dependent imprinting . . . " Larsen, Earnie and Prague, Jane. *Recovering Catholics: What To Do When Religion Comes Between You and God* (San Francisco: HarperCollins, 1992). p. 77.

6. "author John Sanford observes that Dr. Jekyll . . . " Sanford, John. "Dr. Jekyll and Mr. Hyde," *Meeting the Shadow: The Hidden Power of the Dark Side of Human Nature.* Zweig, Connie and Abrams, Jeremiah, eds. (Los Angeles: Jeremy P. Tarcher, Inc., 1990). pp. 29-34.

7. "The human body has lived . . . " *Meeting the Shadow: The Hidden Power of the Dark Side of Human Nature.* Zweig, Connie and Abrams, Jeremiah, editors. (Los Angeles: Jeremy P. Tarcher, 1990). p. 83.

6

Unpacking The God-Box

Remember when I told you that God had sent the
answer to a problem I'd been having? You said,
"Funny how when something good happens, God did
it, but if something bad happens, it's your fault." You
really got to me with that one. I thought I'd truly
come to a new understanding of God, but I suddenly saw that I hadn't changed it much at all.

Vivian

ONE OF THE KEY MOVES IN THE GOD GAME INVOLVES MAKING THE
decision to take apart the God-Box. Usually this involves a recognition
or some kind of awakening. I call these natural interventions. Writing
the meditation on Fear for my book, *Meditations For Compulsive People,* I
began connecting my childhood belief in a punishing God with my own
religiously controlling and abusive behavior in my Anglo-Catholic days
in England. This was when I truly started confronting my own God-Box
that was full of unhealthy beliefs and attitudes, moving towards a more
freeing, multi-cultural God that reflected love and acceptance. Similarly,
my offhand quip to Vivian put her squarely in front of her God-Box.
She saw how, despite many years of hard work and therapy, she still
denied her own involvement in the choices and decisions she made. In
order to confront this denial, she had to find out where it came from. She

had to unpack her God-Box. In this moment, Vivian began playing the God Game in earnest.

Untangling ourselves from the old beliefs and behaviors that stopped us from enjoying our spiritual power is often the most difficult part of the God Game. It involves the process I call "Stop! Look! Change!" First we stop, as a result of some kind of crisis which gets our attention. Then we learn how to look at it. What is it we really believe? Does it serve us? How? Does it enhance us spiritually by adding to our ability to be positive and creative, or is it yet another nail in the God-Box—a belief or behavior which stops us from seeing and using our spiritual power. This is the point at which many people have called my office, or written letters to me, or attended a workshop. Something I said or wrote caught their attention. They then had an opportunity to look at it, either alone or with a therapist, and decide if they want to change. Now it's their move.

Stop! The Pause That Transforms

Throughout our lives, we have many opportunities to stop and then go in a different direction, to transform some aspect of our lives. In these moments, we stop, look at our own pain, and make the decision that we want to change. Making the decision is the important part, for if we truly have not made the decision, we will not be able to make permanent changes. This applies not only to religious issues, but to all areas of our lives when we need to move out of a destructive pattern into a healthier one. We may make a few half-hearted attempts, but only when we decide deep within us that we want to change are we truly able to make our moves.

This was certainly true in my own case. I had an increasing number of embarrassing alcohol-related incidents, whilst experimenting with trying to control my drinking. After having "just one for the road" at a succession of pubs, I was *seeing* one road too many and crashed my car into a tree. I experienced a feeling of standing outside myself, which I had often done before, but never like this. I floated above myself and saw someone I did not like, an angry drunk who had somehow swallowed up the real me. In that moment, I did not want to be that drunk priest whose parishioners were not at all surprised to see sitting bloody and disheveled beside his totaled car. In that moment, I *knew* that I was an alcoholic, and that I wanted to reconnect to the real me again. I had prayed many times for God to help me, to *make* me stop. I'd done my share of bargaining with God—"just get me out of this mess and I swear, I'll never drink again . . . " This time, I "gave my prayers feet" and made the decision to change, to find out what help was available.

Sometimes, just being told what is wrong is all we need in order to stop. Just as I needed to be told I could change, for many of you, all you may need in order to Stop is the awareness that you have a God-Box that is limiting your spiritual growth. I have met many people like Vivian who spent years chasing God and spirituality through therapy, self-help groups and books, and different religions and philosophies, never understanding what was in the way. Sadly, I have also seen people relapsing from addictive, struggling with chronic depression, even committing suicide, because the issues contained in the God-Box were never identified or resolved. I often wonder if knowing about the God-Box might have made a difference. For those of you whose God-Box has led you into addictive and compulsive behavior, your primary efforts may at first be directed towards recovery from those problems. But if, alongside this recovery, you are aware that beneath the addiction, the depression, the dysfunction, lies a God-Box which is likely to be a prime source of your broken spirituality, you will have a much better chance of attaining healthy spirituality much sooner in the recovery process.

For me, understanding that I have a God-Box gives me a direction when I'm feeling frustrated or stuck, or there is a situation which seems to recur. It helps me figure out my part, so I can make productive moves. Is there something about my attitude or response to a situation that has its roots in the God-Box? Have I disconnected from my feelings again? Are some of my core beliefs or unhealthy messages coming back to haunt me? When I stop, I then have the space I need to take a look to see if there is something I need to change. That's why I call these stopping places "transforming moments," because they offer the opportunity to change, to transform some aspect of myself and therefore continue to grow spiritually.

Keep in mind, though, that stopping does not always lead to change. Sometimes, we are simply not ready. Perhaps there are other moves to be made first. Perhaps we have stopped in a place where we just can't see any other way to go. Later, we may discover that other moves we have made have created enough of a shift that we can discover alternatives.

That's what's exciting about playing the God Game. It's not a linear progression, or even a circular one, like ripples from a stone in the water. We move forward, backward, sideways or diagonally across our lives as we play our God Game. Sometimes, we go through a series of stops that take us to that transforming moment where we make the decision to change. As a friend described the years it took him to stop smoking: "Each time I'd try to quit, I got a little more willing the next time. It was sort of like I was willing to be willing to want to stop, then I was willing to want to stop, then I wanted to stop, then I wanted to stop badly enough to really do it for good!" Instead of beating himself up for starting again, he began looking forward to the next stop, having discovered that each one took him closer to that transformative moment when he could make his final decision to change. This is how many of us will begin to tackle our God-Boxes—not in one clean sweep, but bit by bit.

Look! Identifying What's In the God-Box

The first thing to understand is that not everything in our God-Box is totally bad. We will do more transforming than tossing out. Because I travel so much, I think of the God-Box like the suitcase I take on a trip. When I return, some clothing definitely must go to the laundry. Other things just need a good airing. And once in a while, I have to discard items that have become worn out. Before I can decide what to do about them, I have to first look at them. Unpacking my God-Box involves much the same process.

Just as we all have different approaches to packing and unpacking, so we will all have a different approach to identifying what's in our God-Box. Some of you may want to go right to the beginning and look at your childhood concept of God, for that will tell you much about what is in your God-Box. Others will discover that you can't get to that childhood concept without moving some things out of the way—looking at your co-dependency, or the Unhealthy Religious Messages. You might have to work on the fear of even questioning what you were taught about God.

There are no rules, no specific order or sequence for unpacking your God-Box. Some of us have such a tangle that we just have to grab the first loose end and start unraveling it. So even though I'm going to follow the same sequence we used to describe building our God-Box in Chapter Five, don't think you have to follow the same order. Or even use the same processes. Taking a tip from the Twelve Step programs, I'll say that these suggestions are not absolutes. They are meant to serve as guidelines, as ideas to spark your own creativity.

DISCOVERING YOUR CHILDHOOD CONCEPT OF GOD

I suggest starting at the beginning, by tracing how your concept of God evolved. Often, you can find out a lot about your God-Box just by identifying what you believe about God, and where you learned it. As children of God, we have been handed an array of shame and fear-producing rules, regulations, and rituals which formed our image of God. This image of God became our God-Box. If we were raised with taboos about sexuality, a whole lot of fear, shame and judgmentalism is likely to have gone into the God-Box, and our precious sexuality was shed like dirty clothes. If we were taught that other people's needs are to be put ahead of our own, people-pleasing and caretaking go into the God-Box; boundaries and self-worth are left outside. We have put into the God-Box those things which confused, frustrated, angered us. Cast aside are many of the valuable gifts we were given by God: self-esteem, choices, responsibility, feelings, sexuality, acceptance of variety and difference.

To understand the effect that such messages have on children, let's take a minute to look at how children view the world. In an editorial in the *Arkansas Gazette*, titled "Children in the hands of an angry preacher," guest writer William White told of an encounter he had with a man who was describing a kind of abuse of children that no one was talking about. He recounted to White the effect being taken to a religious revival had on him as a child:

> Suddenly I felt guilt and fear for the first time. How could I be guilty of such crimes when I could not remember any of them. I began to doubt what I knew—I was only a child. I was so afraid, I trembled inside. What other terrible things had I done that I didn't know about?
>
> My life was never the same . . . I had nightmares and mental anguish. How could I have been such a terrible person and not known it? . . . What a traumatic crime against children, and it's still going on.[1]

There it is: the fear and terror which lead to perfectionism and control, to religious addiction, to self-destructiveness because we don't know what we did wrong, and thus feel helpless to fix it. But we try. We desperately try.

The gentleman talking to William White said that, before being taken to the revival, he had felt attuned to the universe—part of nature, God, and everything. "Sometimes I could not distinguish myself from my surroundings," he said. "I had no fear, no guilt." White agreed, saying, "A child lives in his imagination, and his world should be secure from the realities of the world."[2]

Many of us have had similar experiences which we may have actually forgotten, or thought we had worked through. Often, these are the experiences which lead to our becoming refugees from religion. We need to unearth them, so we can begin to connect them with the other parts of the God-Box. If you can remember at what age you were first introduced to religion, it may be helpful to list some of the things you were taught—songs, stories, any lessons or rules and whether they were taught by your parents, or through your religion.

One valuable tool I use when I work with people in hospitals and treatment programs is to have them draw their childhood image of God. If you are afraid that your *grown-up* self might get in the way, use your non-dominant hand—your left hand if you are right-handed, and vice-versa. Not having your usual control is an effective means of getting in touch with your little self. Draw a picture of your childhood image of an angry God. Then draw your childhood image of a loving God.

If drawing is difficult, then write about how you saw God as a child. Again, using the non-dominant hand technique is useful for getting in touch with those old memories. The following exercises will help you discover your basic beliefs about God, and how old you were when you developed them.

HOW OLD ARE YOU IN
YOUR RELATIONSHIP WITH GOD?

Ages 0 - 5 Early Childhood

What role did religion play in your family?

__Major focus__Moderate emphasis

__Average__Minimal__None at all

At what age can you recall first hearing about God?

What were you told?

At what age did you first attend Sunday School or begin to receive formal religious training?

Do you remember any particular stories or teachings that made an impression? What were they, and how were you affected?

What were you taught about your body?

What were you taught about your mind (ability to think)?

What were you taught about your feelings?

If you had any questions, did you feel free to ask them?

If you asked, how were your questions received?

What were some of your questions?

What was your image of God?

Ages 6-11 Childhood

What role did religion play in your family?

__Major focus__Moderate emphasis

__Average__Minimal__None at all

What were you taught about God?

What religious rules or messages were you given?

Do you remember any particular stories or teachings that made an impression? What were they, and how were you affected?

What were you taught about your body?

What were you taught about sex?

What were you taught about your mind (ability to think)?

What were you taught about your feelings?

What were you taught about choices, power, and responsibility?

Did you notice any discrepancy between what you were taught was model behavior, and the behavior of your parents or religious teachers? How did you feel about that?

If you had any questions, did you feel free to ask them?

If you asked, how were your questions received?

What were some of your questions?
What was your image of God? Did it change?

Ages 12 -21 Adolescence And Young Adulthood
What role did religion play in your family
__Major focus__Moderate emphasis
__Average__Minimal__None at all
What were you taught about God?
Was it different from the information you were given as a child?
What religious rules or messages were you given?
What were you taught about your body?
What were you taught about sex?
What were you taught about your feelings?
What were you taught about your mind (ability to think)?
What were you taught about choices, power, and responsibility?
Did you notice any discrepancy between what you were taught was
    model behavior, and the behavior of your parents or religious
    teachers? How did you feel about that?
If you had any questions, did you feel free to ask them?
If you asked, how were your questions received?
How did you feel about yourself?
How did you feel about God?
What was your image of God? Did it change?

Now, describe your image of God today. Don't be surprised if you
discover that it is very similar to one or more of the stages in the above
exercises. Most of us suffer a kind of arrested development in our spiritual growth, just as we may have in our emotional and psychological
growth. Finding out how old you are in your relationship with God
may help you go back and recall what you were like at that age—how
you felt about yourself, and how you responded to the world. If you
were an angry, rebellious teenager, you may discover that you have had
the same attitude towards God that you had towards your parents at
the same age. If you find you are five years old in your relationship
with God, you will probably find that your God-Box is full of dependency and helplessness.

IDENTIFYING YOUR CORE BELIEFS

From these exercises and other work, you can identify your core beliefs about God. When you list all the rules, messages, and teachings you ever heard, you will usually start to notice a pattern. When I did these exercises, I noticed several patterns that were perpetuated by nearly all of my childhood experiences. Even as young as ages two and three, I can remember my mother telling me that God would come and take me away from her if I was naughty. Starting at ages five and six, I was taught in Sunday School that God punishes, destroys, or kills people who anger Him.

Around this time, I started hearing what would be a constant litany for the rest of my growing up years: "Take care of your body," which meant I was to be clean and neat in appearance; improve my mind, which meant to study sacred texts and works; and feelings should be directed towards God. This meant that any feelings that I had that came up in church or around the "sacred"—liturgy, theology, religiously inspired art, and drama—were OK. Otherwise, my feelings were to be suppressed. I learned that I was a good boy if I listened, and the only kinds of questions that were okay were the ones that would please family and priests (and therefore, God). From the time I was six years old, most of my social life revolved around religion. I served as an altar boy, and it was my secret goal to always be the "special" boy, the "teacher's pet," in order to avoid punishment and win praise. This pattern has stayed with me all my life in some form or another.

Another pattern that these exercises revealed was a widening distance between me and God. Increasingly, the Church spoke for God, and I interacted with God through the Church. As I said in Chapter Two, just as at home, when I asked my father a question and my mother answered for him, so the Church answered and spoke for God. Until I did these exercises, I had never realized how much my relationship with God and the Church resembles my relationship with my mother. I had a sudden, terrifying thought: When my mother dies, will God die? I wonder if this fear has lurked way down deep since I was a very little boy, for in many ways my mother's authority and God's authority were so deeply linked in my childhood. Of course, when the inevitable comes and my mother passes on, I know that God will not die. I do suspect that my core belief in the distant, punishing God will undergo a final transformation. Understanding how I have linked my mother and God together will help me during the grieving process when the time comes.

This is how doing exercises such as these can help you begin identifying your core beliefs. Remember, these are suggested guidelines only. You may have some other tools and exercises that will help you identify your core beliefs and the unhealthy messages you heard all your life. And you don't have to do it all at once. This is an ongoing process. You'll be discovering parts of your God-Box for a long time. But once you learn to recognize the pieces, you are ready to start transforming them.

Change! Beginning the Transformation

Some of the most powerful moves in the God Game involve learning how to change the way we talk to ourselves, revising the old negative language which says, "I can't; I must not; I should or should not do something." If we have been in a belief system which tells us not to doubt or question, we must learn how to evaluate and think for ourselves, and to express those thoughts and opinions appropriately. If we have buried our sexuality in a tomb of guilt, shame and "thou shalt nots," then we must gently uncover it and befriend it so that we treat our sexual selves with respect and dignity. If we have used religious rules and rituals as a substitute for making choices, we may need to come to a new understanding of their place in our lives, so we can reclaim choice and responsibility.

This is why we need to be able to identify our core beliefs and the messages that reinforce them, so we can begin to transform and sometimes, even discard them. This is the process of "Stop! Look! Change!" Joan Borysenko calls it "Spiritual ReVision"—reviewing religious beliefs to see if they have been spiritually damaging or spiritually nurturing, then discovering a new vision of what spirituality is. It is the process of moving away from thinking that spirituality is a *concept* of God, and moving towards understanding spirituality as *experiencing* God.[3]

One way to begin that process is to write down what exactly we don't like, don't agree with, or somehow want to change about our image of God, and why. Then write down the qualities we would like God to have, if we could choose how God might look. Sometimes, people find that they need to abandon or change the gender of God.

My friend Anna told me about an exercise she did in a workshop, in which they were asked to imagine the conversation they might have had with God on the eve of their birth.

"First, I ran through all the images of God—from the angry scary God to a twinkly grandfather God and realized I didn't like any of them. So I decided to try a female image that showed all the qualities I wanted God to have: nurturing, warmth, and acceptance. The most wonderful face I could think of was the late actress Colleen Dewhurst. She had such a warm, earth-mother quality about her, a great strength, and that incredible smile that just seemed to light up a room. So that's what I decided God looked like."

For Anna, this was just the beginning of the journey away from the God-Box. Today, she considers herself mid-way into the process. For her, God is no longer an entity. She shuns churches and religions, choosing carefully the kinds of spiritual beliefs she opens herself to as she seeks ways to discover the presence of God within her. "Putting a new face" on God was one of her moves into the process of creating an adult relationship with God.

God Doesn't "Get" Us—We "Get" God

You may find that creating your own personal image of God will help you begin to move away from the beliefs that reinforce powerlessness and the feeling of being a pawn in God's great Game with the Universe. Believing that we are pawns in some Universal scheme means that we always believe something else is in control of our lives. This is the concept of "game" as the object of a hunt. Our choices, actions and responsibilities are therefore all in response to this external control. We spend our energy trying to elude God's wrath, so that God will not "get us," not hunt us down and punish us.

In *Guilt is the Teacher, Love is the Lesson*, Joan Borysenko notes that, although it was funny on the TV show *Maude*, "God will get you" isn't funny when people really believe it. In her work as a therapist, Borysenko has counseled numerous people who believed God would get them, or had already done so. She chronicles the case of Peter, whose critical, abusive parents raised him with a great Catholic fear of mortal sin. As a child, he was required to confess to his priest, who doled out harsh penances, and he also had to confess to his father, who would beat him until his buttocks bled. To avoid such dual punishments, he became adept at lying, calculating how much to tell the priest so that he wouldn't look like he was a saint, but wouldn't be abused either.

At age 45, he had long considered himself an atheist, but after contracting herpes during an extramarital affair, he suffered a resurgence of his religious guilt. Catching herpes was bad enough, but the lesions always broke out on his buttocks, reminding him of his childhood agonies. Though he would have sworn his belief in a punishing, angry God had long been abandoned, Borysenko helped him see that he had only set it aside. She showed him that he was suffering from two cases of mistaken identity: his identification of himself as a hopeless, worthless sinner, and his identity of God as an unforgiving, punitive destroyer.[4]

The case of Peter is an excellent example of how the God-Box remains firmly attached to us, hampering our ability to move away from beliefs we know have harmed us. In Peter's case, the harsh penances doled out by his priest only validated the cruel messages taught by his parents. Small wonder he could not escape his belief that God would get him, when the person he was taught represented God on earth stood in brutal judgment over him.

This is one of the most common forms of clergy abuse —not only the harsh punitiveness itself, but the fact that a "man of God" was meting out the punishment only reinforced the unhealthy message that God is angry and vengeful. This is an example of how, when God is used as a weapon, it is easy for people to get confused about what is actually hurting them—the weapon, or the person using it. In Peter's mind, abandoning religion and an intellectual belief in God should have freed him from his belief that God would get him. But as Borysenko pointed out, religion and God weren't the real problems; rather, his perceptions of his relationship to God are what caused his pain. In showing him that his basic beliefs about himself and God were mistaken, she opened the door that would allow him to get out of his God-Box.

Changing our perceptions about God and our relationship to God is not easy. It involves the willingness to change—making the decision that we want to change our beliefs. Once we've made the decision, there are a variety of tools we can use to start our "Spiritual ReVision." One of the most useful and versatile tools we can use is a technique called "reframing," which helps us revise our core beliefs.

REFRAMING: TRANSFORMING OLD BELIEFS

Reframing is, literally, putting a new frame around a belief or behavior that allows you to either change the behavior, or change your belief about it. Here's an example of one method of reframing: A woman who was participating in a reframing workshop admitted to being obsessive about footprints on her carpet. She nagged her family endlessly, trying to keep them from walking on the carpet. They could put up with the rest of her "clean-freak" eccentricities, but her war on footprints in the carpet drove them nuts. We're not talking about dirt and mud here, just the ordinary dents even bare feet can make in a nice carpet.

In the workshop, the facilitator had this woman visualize her carpet pristinely free of footprints. Then she was asked to look at that lovely clean space and see that it meant that she was absolutely alone—all of her loved ones were far away. This of course made the woman feel terrible. Next she was asked to visualize a lot of footprints on the carpet, and to recognize that the footprints meant that her loved ones were nearby. In this way, the woman learned to reframe what the footprints meant to her. Instead of representing failure as a house-keeper, she learned, after a lot of practice, to see them as signs of success—of providing a loving home in which her family felt welcome and comfortable.[5]

What this woman learned to do was to script a different story about what footprints in the carpet meant to her. You can use this technique to revise some of the unhealthy messages you received as a child. If you were taught, for instance, that showing anger was bad, you can change the story you tell yourself about what is wrong with expressing feelings. You will never get the hang of the healthy expression of feelings if you don't first make it OK to express them at all. So reframing becomes a powerful tool in helping us reclaim the parts of ourselves that got disconnected as a result of our God-Box.

RECLAIMING YOUR "SHADOW"

Perhaps you are already aware of how your God-Box has pulled you apart. You may already know that you have difficulty making choices, or expressing your feelings, or taking risks and responsibility. You may know the sources of your shame and guilt. If not, the "How Old Are You" exercises may also provide clues as to where you have disconnected. One thing that immediately jumped out for me was the way in which I learned to mask my feelings. As a priest, and even now as a lecturer and educator, there's often a difference between the "Real" Leo and the "Official" Leo. Having had to mask my feelings all through childhood created the "Shadow" side of Leo—the parts that secretly said to myself, "This is stupid. This minister is a jerk. These people are inept." In my youth, and even sometimes today, I gained a reputation for being arrogant, for I often hid my insecurity and fear behind a facade of superiority. When I am tired and afraid I will make a mistake, I "turn myself off" and people rightly perceive me as cold. Much of my work in embracing my own Shadow side has to do with letting go of control and learning to feel and express my feelings honestly and appropriately.

Healing Our Sexuality

As we learned in Chapter Five, the part of us that most frequently gets disconnected or abandoned, besides our feelings, is our sexuality. Healing and reclaiming our wounded sexuality often requires a big leap for many people, for it involves the willingness to believe that sexual shame is a human invention. I believe that *God never intended for human sexuality to be shameful.* Equally important, we must recognize that clergy have no more special connection to God than any other people. Understanding that God did not give any clergy or religious authority permission to cause shame and guilt is a key step toward confronting and healing the wounds of religious abuse, and most especially, the damage to our sexuality done in the name of God. From my work with other survivors of religious abuse, I know that this is the hardest hurdle you will face, because it requires tremendous courage to examine and discard the unhealthy religious messages that fill the God-box.

This is an especially important area for women, and for gay men and lesbians. The religious-based messages about the secondary, inferior status of women, as well as the distortion of scripture to persecute homosexuality, has done very great harm. I believe these messages are the source of so much co-dependency in women, and have sowed the seeds of a deep-seated self-hate in homosexuals. At the very least, these kinds of messages hold both women and gays back from claiming their spiritual power, for we live in a society that is still infested with unhealthy attitudes.

Both women and gays share a common bond in that the Spiritual Value of Truth is often denied them. They are not allowed to be

REAL. We have all heard the complaint that a man who stands up for himself is considered assertive; the woman who equally sets her boundaries is aggressive, a man-hater—any number of sexist slurs. Yet there are some Biblical stories about women standing up for themselves. Despite the fact that a good number of women in the *Bible* are portrayed as either impossibly loyal or as harlots and temptresses, alongside these stories are examples of the sheer persistence of women in scripture.

It is this same persistence that has finally broken the all-male barriers of the priesthood. Although the first women to enter the clergy were given male role models, and in order to survive, they had to adopt the male attitudes of their brother clergy or they seldom made it through seminary, that is changing. The women pioneers in these areas are forging new ground. As they reclaim their own personal power, in many ways, they begin transforming the stereotypes and myths about what is feminine, as well as creating new roles for claiming spiritual power. The women who follow them now have their own feminine role models, and that influence will eventually provide greater balance amongst the priesthood at large.

Similarly, I work with many gays and lesbians who try desperately to create healthy relationships, not realizing that part of the problem is that their concept of a "healthy relationship" is based on heterosexual role models. While there are many common denominators between heterosexual and gay relationships, trying to live according to "straight" rules often leads to depression and despair. How can we expect gays and lesbians to love a God whom they are told hates and despises who they are? How can they be REAL, and stand in their own spiritual Truth?

That's why reframing old beliefs is essential for homosexuals. I find that the gays and lesbians who have built enduring, healthy relationships are the ones who have refashioned or abandoned the traditional role models and created their own set of guidelines. They have moved out of the religious co-dependency that demands that they give up who they are, and instead become courageously, spiritually REAL.

I'll say it again: All women, gay or straight, have been sexually abused by religious teachings that brand them as inferior based only on their gender. Any form of sexual abuse leaves severe spiritual wounds, and it is worse when the abuse is done in the name of God.

Adding to the pain is often the collection of religious messages that says that God takes care of the good and punishes the evil. "Where was God?" That tormenting question. The answer is that God was where God has always been: right here with us. Sometimes, as I work with patients in treatment programs, or people who come to me as a priest, I ask them to play a little "What if" game:

- What if the people who told you God saves those who are good enough were confused and didn't exactly understand what salvation means?

- What if salvation means having the strength and courage to walk through pain?

- What if grace comes with the willingness to trust?

- What if the presence of pain and injustice and all the other imperfections in the world exist not as a test of our "goodness" but are the price of the spiritual freedom to choose?

THE SPIRITUAL GIFT OF CHOICE

The single most disempowering rule in the dysfunctional human family of God is the taboo against asking questions. If we never questioned, or took risks, we would still think the earth was flat, and the center of the universe. There would be no music, art, science, or technology. We are called "higher beings" because we have the capacity to think and reason, yet our religions seem hell-bent on keeping us from doing too much of that. The distrust inherent in the taboos against questioning reinforce the feelings of childishness, as well as feeding the adolescent rebellion against authority.

My friend Father Ralph and I have a running dialogue about questioning and its relationship to faith. Ralph absolutely believes that if we "make a space for God, then God will come in." Sort of like a religious twist on the "If you build it, they will come," theme in the movie *Field of Dreams*. If we invite God in, God will come, and somehow change the situation. I told Ralph about Lisa, a young woman who was carjacked and brutally raped by four men. She had a St. Christopher medal in her car, and kept praying over and over for God to make it stop. I asked Ralph if that meant that Lisa had not made a good enough place for God, or that God had declined the invitation. "Leo, people don't want to ask those kinds of questions. It might be seen as doubting God, or questioning God's activity in the world."

Father Ralph is so totally tangled up in religion's God-Box that he cannot see that there could be a difference between questioning what religion has traditionally taught, and questioning God. I asked him how he would counsel Lisa if she were a member of his own parish. He shuddered; the idea clearly terrified him. "I would pray with her for God to help her forgive these sinners, and to invite God in to help her heal her pain."

"But what if God doesn't come? She begged God to stop the rape and He didn't. So what will happen if she makes a place and God doesn't come?" Ralph has no answer. Part of unpacking religion's God-Box will involve educating the Father Ralphs of this world that, even if they are not ready to abandon that belief in their own personal lives, such beliefs are no longer appropriate, and indeed, are abusive.

As I spoke with Lisa, seeking to help her work through her pain and rage, I asked her if she was willing to consider some different concepts of what she'd been taught, as a means to help in her healing. "What if the people who told you that God would keep these things from happening were passing on beliefs that are way, way out of date? What if God works in our lives in a variety of ways? We know that bad things happen to good people. Is it possible to find God in the moves we make to deal with the hard times in life?" In suggesting these questions to her, I hoped that she might begin to understand the difference between what people tell her God says or wants, and what she can discover about God within herself.

There is a difference between a negative, victimized doubt that says "This won't work; I can't; we're wrong and something bad will happen," and a healthy doubt that permits questioning and dialogue with God. I believe part of our spiritual freedom stems from the ability to question, examine and make our own decisions. Questioning God's activity in the world allows us to appreciate all that God has made available to us. Yes, that includes pain, illness and hardship. Yet we have many scriptural examples of people questioning God. Look at Jesus' long night in Gethsemene, or the agony of his trial and crucifixion. Are these not scripts for "questioning" God? Where does this leave choice, and responsibility, if we cannot question and doubt?

OVERCOMING GUILT AND SHAME

Alongside Fear, guilt and shame keep us stuck in the God-Box. As you identify your core beliefs and begin to reclaim some of your disowned self, you may find that you will have to battle your way through much shame. There are many excellent tools that help you reframe the things you feel shameful about: affirmations, meditations, little rituals and ceremonies. Something I've become aware of is how often the affirmations, and even the songs and hymns we use to inspire us contain little seeds of disempowerment. I can't tell you how often I hear people affirm, "I am a precious child of God," without realizing that the image they get from this is of a little child. Yes, this is important for healing the wounds of the inner child within you. But you also want to heal the adult child of God. I am still my mother's son, and yes, there is still within me the little boy who's got his Mum all tangled up with God and the Church. But there is also the adult Leo who needs to affirm his grown-up relationship with God. If I don't affirm my adult relationship with God, I shall never be able to show that little boy how to grow up and become a powerful player with a God who is his friend, and not a scary Bogeyman.

Sometimes, we may need to give ourselves permission to change one or two words in a hymn or prayer in order to transform it. There are so many scriptural passages and hymns which are very beloved, but which, unfortunately, reinforce helplessness, and reliance on a "fix-it" God. Yet they have provided genuine comfort and hope for many years; I wouldn't want to see them totally abandoned. My friend Anna, in her process of rebuilding her spiritual beliefs "from the ground up," found that she still loves the tunes of many of her favorite hymns from childhood. Anna discovered that, by simply changing some of the words, hymns like "Amazing Grace" retain their beauty and spiritual inspiration. "It's not even the words so much as it is the attitude and my own understanding of what they mean that makes a difference," she says.

All she did was change the words "saved a wretch like me" to "guides a friend like me." To her, the hymn then becomes a celebration of the miracle of co-creatorship, and specifically, of her recovery from addictions and sexual abuse. "You bet I was lost—lost to myself, blind to my issues, and to my strengths. You say it all the time, Leo— what is grace but acceptance and love of self that allows others and God into our lives? And when you never believed it possible, to find that self-acceptance is pretty amazing grace!"

Sometimes, reframing involves taking a break from traditional religion or from certain practices such as meditating or attending workshops and retreats, in order to create a safe space for a new understanding of God to take root. Claire, whom we met in Chapter Four, tried a succession of churches and grew more frustrated and despairing. She truly did not want to abandon the sense of roots and connection she found in traditional religion. But in order to get clear about what she really wanted from religion, she needed to take a break. After a time away, she joined a group of people who met in each other's homes to share the positive things they found in religion—a favorite hymn, a prayer. Taking this break has allowed Claire to discover that what she really wanted from church was the sense of connectedness, belonging and family. "It's really neat, Leo. I never knew we could actually find something positive about religion!" Claire says that her next move is to find a way to feel connected in a church without feeling that she has to embrace all the doctrine and dogma. For now, she is content to enjoy her support group.

I want to repeat again: There are no hard and fast rules for reframing, reclaiming and transforming our spiritual power. My guidelines for myself are: Do they make sense in the context of my life? Does this enhance my connection to myself, or does it cause me to feel embarrassed and ashamed? In time, you will evolve your own special way to dialogue with God. There are many excellent workbooks that will help you identify your core issues and begin to resolve them. I have listed the ones I found useful in the Resources section at the end of the book. These are by no means all, and just because I found them helpful doesn't mean you must. Reclaiming spiritual power means you have the freedom to decide for yourself what is best for you in creating your partnership with God.

Cleaning Out Religion's God-Box

What is the purpose of calling the Refugees from Religion home, if that religious home is still riddled with abuse and remains unsafe? Religious leaders and organizations bear responsibility to look at how many traditions, dogmas, and doctrines increasingly make religion unsafe—how it damages self-esteem by robbing people of their ability to fully realize their unique specialness and individuality. For religion to truly become a safe harbor, religious organizations must cease to see themselves as the only *place* to which people can run for God's care and protection, and instead, become the *process* by which people learn to keep themselves safe. The challenge, for religion and its refugees, is to unite in a "Spiritual Re-Vision" which nurtures and celebrates a mature, adult partnership with God that involves choice, responsibility and personal empowerment.

This spiritual revision is possible *only if religious organizations themselves are willing to change.* Just as individuals must be willing to recognize and confront the God-Box, so religion must be willing to confront its own dysfunction.

We are operating with an outdated religious structure that no longer serves us. In order to have a spiritually healthy Twenty-First Century, we must overhaul the traditional services and texts of modern religion. If the language of religion fosters dependency, powerlessness and sexism, then we must change it. Like a tree that is overgrown, we must prune out the dead parts of religion in order to save it. Yes, like a newly pruned tree, religion may look a little barren for a while, until it sprouts new growth. But to avoid this drastic action risks letting it die altogether.

MOVING THE PRIESTHOOD FROM SPIRITUAL CONTROL TO SPIRITUAL GUIDANCE

One thing that needs to be reframed is the idea that the clergy are somehow more connected to God, more spiritually astute, than the rest of us. Traditionally, priests and ministers in many churches and universities assert that they speak for God. This approach needs to be replaced with a concept of *spiritual guidance*, rather than absolute authoritarianism which claims to interpret what God or the Bible actually means. God does not need an interpreter. We might sometimes need facilitators to help us communicate with ourselves and with God, but not in the way clergy have been accustomed to controlling the dialogue.

Father Ralph represents the priestly old guard. He maintains the paternalistic, authoritarian attitude I saw in many priests in my university days—the kind who view their congregations as a pack of sniveling children and treat them as such. Yet this is how Ralph was trained. I have watched Ralph struggle to cope with the changes within the Episcopal Church, seen his pain and bewilderment. For, even though Ralph bears responsibility for not changing within himself, he is not receiving any support from the Church in helping him cope with the changes.

While the younger clergy may be learning new concepts and approaches, the Father Ralphs are left to cope as best they can. Many cling harder to the old ways, trying to make them work. Some leave altogether. Part of cleaning out religion's God-Box must involve re-educating existing clergy, helping them move away from patterns and styles of priestly governance the Church itself has created. In many ways, the Church and its congregations are changing right out from under the older clergy, literally pulling the rug out from under the old system and expecting the old guard to just blindly follow along. This is almost cruel, for many of these priests, like Ralph, spent thirty or forty years being praised for doing something they are now criticized for, and they don't understand. I believe religious administrative structures need to pay more attention to the emotional and psychological well-being of its clergy by offering retreats and seminars designed to help make the transition through the changes, for how else can they guide their congregations through those changes?

The old concept of the clergy as shepherds leading a flock needs to be abandoned. This concept is responsible for the passivity and victimization so prevalent in religions today. It fosters abuses by a rigid authoritarian clergy accustomed and trained to herd a blindly obedient flock. Today's clergy need to be moderators, facilitators in our dialogue with God. A new breed of clergy could teach how to tap into the spiritual power of God within us, starting with ways to rewrite scriptures so that they retain their spiritual vision, but with the old sexist, disempowering language taken out.

REFRAMING THE LANGUAGE OF DISEMPOWERMENT

Like biological parents who are being taught healthier ways to talk to their children, Mother Church needs to learn that the language she has been using for centuries often creates shame, fear, low self-esteem and helplessness. In parenting classes, people learn how to separate the behavior, to say "That's not a good thing to do," rather than saying the child is bad for doing it. Unfortunately, Mother Church constantly seems to be telling us we are bad at our core, rather than explaining why certain behavior might hurt us or others. As a result, we never learn a healthy basis for making choices which is essential for spiritual empowerment.

Sometimes, reframing may require us to really overhaul the language of scripture, to move it away from disempowerment and helplessness to a more powerful illustration of moves we can make. Let's look at the Twenty-Third Psalm, which is one of the most beloved passages in the Bible. It is meant to give strength and hope, but when you take it apart line by line, *without creative interpretation*, it becomes a prime example of how the language of religion keeps us feeling powerless, waiting for God to take care of us.

> The Lord is my shepherd, I shall not want;
> He makes me lie down in green pastures.
> He leads me beside still waters;
> He restores my soul.
> He leads me in the paths of righteousness
> for His name's sake.
> Even though I walk through the valley of the shadow of death,
> I fear no evil;
> for Thou art with me;
> Thy rod and Thy staff,
> they comfort me.
> Thou preparest a table before me in the presence of my enemies;
> Thou anointest my head with oil,
> my cup overflows.
> Surely, goodness and mercy will follow me
> all the days of my life;
> and I shall dwell in the house of the Lord forever.

As traditionally written, God is doing everything for us or to us: God makes us lie down in green pastures; God leads us, restores us, prepares a table for us. What is our part? Where is our involvement? As it has been traditionally worded, this Psalm does not reflect any interaction or participation on our part, other than a willingness to be led. Most important, it perpetuates the idea that good things are going to happen to us all our days if we follow our Shepherd. Often, when I counsel people who are struggling with spiritual confusion, they point to the Twenty-Third Psalm as a source of their feelings of betrayal and abandonment by God, because the "goodness and mercy" it seems to promise has eluded them.

As I became aware of how religious language disempowers us, I took a hard look at the prayers and readings we were using in both my morning service and the monthly Recovery Mass. As an example of spiritual empowerment, we re-worded the Twenty-Third Psalm so that it reflected a more involved partnership with God:

> God is my friend. What more could I want?
> God sits with me in the quiet times of my life,
> God explores with me the meaning of my life.
> God calls me forth as a whole person.
> Even though I walk along paths of pain, prejudice, hatred
> and depression, my fears are quieted because God is with me.
> God's words and thoughts challenge me.
> God causes me to be sensitive to the needs of mankind,
> then lifts up opportunities for serving.
> God's confidence stretches me.
> Surely love shall be mine to share throughout my life,
> and I shall be sustained by God's concern forever.

Yes, there are people who are actually afraid of this revised version, who subliminally fear that God is going to get them, or me, for supposedly tampering with the *Bible*. Some refuse to say it, or simply never come back. For others, it is has been a slow process of coming to understand the concept of spiritual empowerment. We close the celebration with a meditation I wrote especially for that service:

> Oh God, you have given me the power to determine my life. May I remember to include myself in my amends. May I never be afraid to reveal my anger or concern to those who have abused me. Today I know that I can never love you or others fully and healthily until I begin to love myself. With you as my Partner and Co-Creator I am discovering all that is lovable and powerful within me. Thank you for guiding me as I reclaim myself.

This is how we can begin the process of revising the language of disempowerment, as well as moving the priesthood away from its authoritarianism and control and into the role of guides to spiritual *experience* rather than as dictators of spiritual concepts.

Moving away from perpetuating a belief in the infallibility of religious authority is one step in cleaning out the sexism and sexually damaging part of religion's God-Box. The very taboo against questioning creates the perfect environment for abuse to breed. According to a therapist who treats victims of ritual abuse, sexual perpetrators often use religious-affiliated schools and kindergartens as a screen for wholesale sexual abuse, precisely because of the blind, unquestioning trust that is placed in such facilities.[6] Religion has done its job well, teaching people not to question or challenge its authority. Until very recently, clergy and the religiously addicted were free to do as they liked, whether it was sexual abuse or financial exploitation, knowing they had a powerful ally in all the dogma and doctrine about sin, sex and secrecy. As the Rev. Marie Fortune sums it up in her book, *Is Nothing Sacred?*:

> First, the church is myopic about the problem of abuse by
> clergy. Although the problem has existed for years, the church
> remains unprepared to address it. Second, the power of the
> pastoral role is a power seldom acknowledged, particularly in
> denominations with a strong congregational polity. Third, the
> familial model of church congregational life is assumed . . . as it
> is in many churches. When the family serves as the model for
> interaction, then incest is a possibility within the church family
> just as it is within other families. These three aspects, common to
> church life, made it possible for a pastor who was a sex offender
> to carry out his activities with little fear of ever being caught.[7]

Fortune's book is a fascinating case study of a manipulative and exploitative pastor, the women he abused, and the damage done to both the women and the congregation by the church's inability to handle such abuse. In it, she challenges all churches to look at how ill-prepared they are to handle cases of unethical conduct.

If the Church still chooses to see itself as the family of God, then it must cease its dysfunctional denial and put in place clearly defined tools for dealing with the problem. First, a standard of clergy ethics similar to those for physicians and therapists must be established—not within each denomination or faith, but across the board. No clergyperson of any faith—Christian, Jewish, Buddhist, New Age or Muslim—who molests children should ever be allowed back in a position where any contact with children or families is possible. Period. If this means defrocking, disordination or some other form of removing them from active ministry, then it must be done.

Perhaps clergy should be licensed the same way physicians and therapists are licensed and supervised. No longer is it sufficient to go to school and earn a degree, then never add to formal clerical training. Clergy should be required to obtain ongoing education, a certain number of continuing education credits annually, which is standard procedure for therapists and other professional caregivers.

Second, each church should have clearly defined steps for dealing with sexual abuse, sexual harassment and child molestation. In my church, we had all the staff fingerprinted. What I did not know is that merely fingerprinting people isn't enough. In order to assure that the children and adults in our care are safe from known offenders, we must request that the fingerprints be checked by a number of agencies: local and state law enforcement, as well as the FBI. I assumed all those agencies are in communication with each other. I was shocked to learn that these agencies frequently don't communicate with each other unless specifically asked to do so. This is a lesson for me on empowerment— not just blindly trusting that the so-called authority figures will take care of me. The laws vary from state to state, so it is up to each church to discover what those laws are, and how to incorporate them into their own procedures for prevention, and if necessary, prosecution of sexual abuse or other abuses.

Third, churches need to know where to send clergy for treatment of whatever problems they may be having. After my drunken car crash, my Bishop knew just where to refer me for help. Had he not known how to do this, I might have continued on at the cost of someone else's life, or my own.

Fourth, and most difficult, religion needs to take a long, hard look at what it has been teaching all these thousands of years, to see how its language and liturgy disempower people and set up the abuses. Certainly the Catholic Church must re-examine not just its position on priestly celibacy and birth control, but its stand on sex and sexuality in general.

Unpacking the God-Box will take us many years. It is time to create a body of religious teachings and doctrine which truly reflect and affirm the special relationship which exists between ourselves and God. My hope is that it will become a partnership between the organization of religion itself and the refugees who have disconnected from it. As I

noted in Father Ralph's case, the Church has already begun to change.
We do have women clergy. More and more, gays and lesbians are being
welcomed into mainstream religions. Clergy are being educated differently, and those who need help with addictions and depression are finding it easier to receive treatment. I am not the only priest who is striv-
ing to guide people to choice, self-power and spiritual responsiveness.
Increasingly, clergy are being included in the professional caregiving
networks previously reserved for therapists and addictions professionals.
While there is much more work to be done, I don't want to discount the
changes that are being made. It is not easy to change beliefs and teachings that are encased in centuries of traditions, doctrine and rituals. But
we are doing it, with each powerful move we make in the God Game.

NOTES

1. "Suddenly I felt guilt and fear . . . " White, William. *Arkansas Gazette*.

2. "A child lives in his imagination . . . " ibid.

3. "Joan Borysenko calls it 'Spiritual Re-Vision' . . . " Borysenko, Joan. *Guilt is the Teacher, Love is the Lesson*. (New York: Warner Books, Inc., 1990). p. 124.

4. "She chronicles the case of Peter . . . " ibid.

5. "A woman who was participating in a reframing workshop . . . " Bander, Richard and Grinder, John. *Reframing: Neuro-Linguistic Programming and the Transformation of Meaning*. (Moab, Utah: Real People Press, 1982).

6. "According to a therapist . . . " Hudson, Pamela. *Ritual Child Abuse: Discovery, Diagnosis and Treatment*. (Saratoga, CA: R & E Publishers, 1991). p. 21.

7. "First, the church is myopic . . . " Fortune, Marie M. *Is Nothing Sacred? The Story of a Pastor, the Women He Sexually Abused, and the Congregation He Nearly Destroyed*. (San Francisco: HarperCollins, 1989). p. 99.

7

Moving Into A Healthy Relationship With God

GOD IN THE ODD

"God punishes disobedient children."
I heard that.
That was the message I heard.
In my home.
In my church.
From my grandmother.
Anger.

As a child, I lived in terror:
I was told God the Father sees everything.
Did He keep notes?
Would He punish me?
Would He punish my family?
A hostage in life.
Fear.

God was my Bogeyman.
Would He come for me in the night?
Creep into my bedroom,
tell me I was a sinner,
separate me from my family,
condemn me to hell?
Shame. . . .

Then I found alcohol: . . .
Disaster.
Intervention: A precious moment.
Recovery.

"Discover God as you understand Him."
But my understanding was judgment.
A God who is angry.
A God who condemns the unsaved.
Frustration.

GOD SAYS:
What about re-thinking ME?
You are re-thinking everything else.
Find ME in creation.
Discover ME in dance,
discover ME in animals;
even hugs.

Gamble on your instincts.
The Emperor's new clothes:
Things are not always what they seem.
Sex can be abused.
Alcohol can be abused.
Food can be abused.
Why not God?
Discover God in the Odd.

My message was to create power;
never shame.
Let the child in you play.
Let the child in you dance.
Let the child in you sing.
Those who are unsure must question.
The doubter needs to caution.
The thinker must explore new territory.
Rejoice in your difference.
Discover ME in the odd.

I REPLY:
You are in the odd.
You are in the ordinary:
Jogging,
humor,
relationships,
animals.
In creation, You are revealed.

— FATHER LEO BOOTH
Meditations For Compulsive People

As a child, I was taught to fear God. As a teenager, I both feared God, yet desperately wanted to love God. Unable to resolve the conflict between my childhood image of God and the yearning I felt for a sense of safety and nurture in God's arms, I fell in love instead with the power, control, and majesty of the church. When my treatment for alcoholism also intervened in my religious abuse, my moves were about discovering God in all of creation, and most of all, within me. Now my moves are aimed at deepening and strengthening my partnership with God. It has been a process of gradually moving away from that "Bogeyman" relationship with God into a comfortable relationship with God that is a rich and empowered partnership.

By now you know that the answer to the question, "Why can't I get it?" is that you've always had spirituality. God has always been in your life. You may not have known how to recognize God's presence in your life, or how to activate your own spirituality. Many of our spiritual moves are about learning to discover "God in the Odd" and ordinary places of life. The moves we make ripple through our lives, shifting, lifting, transforming. We make many kinds of moves—some practical, some geographical, some theological or religious. Some of our moves are huge and fraught with crisis; others are so small we might not notice them. But all are spiritual. When we can recognize the spiritual power in all our moves, we are moving closer in our relationship with God. Like any other relationship, our relationship with God is ever-changing. We are always moving into our relationship with God. It's a fluid process that widens and deepens the more we move with it.

This came home to me not long ago, in one of the richest, most sweetly poignant experiences I've had in years. On one of my lecture trips, I had some free time in my schedule and decided to take a walk and explore the city. I rarely get to see more of the places I visit than the airport and a hotel or hospital, so this was a treat. I wandered into a very old Episcopal church, one of the oldest in the Southwest. Obviously very traditionally Anglican, this church still employed the old *Book of Common Prayer* rather than the modernized one. Sitting in the cool, wooden pews, I was instantly transported to my youth, to the days in which I took great refuge and comfort in the ancient liturgies and rituals of my faith. Although today I no longer agree with much of what is written there, for a time, I was able to connect to the boy I had been, to his fears, his hopes, confusions, pain, and joys.

In that moment, I strengthened my relationship with myself, in letting young Leo tell his story of how it felt to be a fourteen-year-old boy afire with the mystery and romance of his church. The adult Leo no longer takes the same kind of comfort from those rituals and liturgies, but I was able to connect to, and honor, that part of me that had been sustained and nourished by them. I left after my brief visit to my young self feeling renewed and serene. It was not the church itself that was sacred, but the feelings, the connection, the relationship that created the sacred moment.

Until that time, I had been feeling almost defensive about remaining in the priesthood, given the degree to which I have come to challenge and confront the unhealthy aspects of religion. But in that empowering moment, I discovered that I do not want to become another refugee from religion. I do not want to join the distinguished ranks of former priests such as Matthew Fox, James Kavanaugh, the Berrigans and others who were driven out of a system that does not tolerate criticism and change. From that moment of recognition, a whole array of moves suddenly became apparent. New options floated up from the stew of choices and indecision that had been quietly bubbling within me for a while. With those options came a more clearly defined direction.

This is what an empowered, adult relationship with God can look like. I did not enter that little church to contemplate my life. I wasn't "carrying my burdens" to God in prayer. I was just delighted to see such a quaint gem amid the modern-day urban sprawl. Yet it became an opportunity for "stillness prayer," that time of communion with God in the truest sense of the word. In allowing myself to connect with the boy I had been, to feel his feelings, I made the small move that opened the door to bigger moves.

Making Our Moves

What is a move? Does it have to feel positive? Are we supposed to feel special when we make one? There are many shades of meaning to the word move. There is the kind of move that gets us out of the way of something, or we move something out of our way. Then there is the sense of being moved, as in responding mentally, emotionally or physically to something, as I did in the little church. There is moving that takes us somewhere different, as in moving into a new house. We have so many ways to move! And in each kind of move, we have a variety of ways in which to activate and involve the Spiritual Values.

In the old days, I thought of spiritual action as kneeling in prayer, studying scripture, or doing acts of charity. I really had put spirituality out in the "ethers," in that great "someplace" where Noble Deeds count as spirituality. There's nothing wrong with those, unless you think they are the *only* spiritual moves you are allowed to make. Today, I don't restrict spirituality to the ethers! Instead, I am learning ways to bring it practically and demonstrably to earth.

When I am asked how I learned to make my moves as a player in the God Game, I point to the example set by Jesus and other great spiritual leaders. This is "The Way" that shows us how to make similar moves. For Christians and non-Christians alike, Jesus can be a powerful role model for how to activate a spiritual life. He was a *protester* who dared to chastise the Pharisees. He was a *radical*, teaching that the Sabbath was made for man, not for God, which was the exact opposite of what was believed at the time. He was a *nurturer*, inviting the little children to come to him, quietly, and sometimes even reluctantly healing those in need. Jesus was a great *visionary;* he pointed straight at the future when he said, "In my house are many mansions," no doubt foreseeing a time when the earth would be filled with such great diversity. Most of all, he was a *motivator*, urging his disciples forward by telling them, "Greater things than I have done, you will do."

I find that most of the people who are my role models share common traits of being radical visionaries—not just Jesus, but Gandhi, Martin Luther King, Charlie Chaplin, and Oscar Wilde. Nor are my role models limited to famous icons. There are many extraordinary "ordinary" people like my friend Anna and others who continually challenge and motivate me. In 1977, I would never have seen it, much less admitted it, but today, I look back at old Harry and see the same Christ-like qualities. Who else but a radical visionary would have had the insight to look inside smug, self-righteous Father Leo and say, "You're full of shit—but you can change!"

In that pivotal moment, Harry challenged me to move from being a spiritual pawn to a powerful player in the God Game. From then on, the moves were up to me. First, I had to get sober. This is an example of moving something out of our way. Sometimes, what we need to move is a set of beliefs or a way of thinking that stops us from making other moves we really want to make. This is where the technique of reframing comes into play, for reframing is simply telling ourselves a new story about a belief or event. In telling the new story, we get to open the door to new responses, and from the responses, comes clarity of choice. The new story about Leo was that he could change. This opened the door to many new stories—and to new insights into old ones, which happened when I sat in that old church and let my young self tell his story.

STORY MOVES

Creating a "new story" offers us a variety of moves that allow us to activate or incorporate the Spiritual Values in our lives. We can reclaim many "disowned parts" such as sexuality, self-esteem, or our ability to think and question. We can make powerful moves into acceptance, forgiveness, balance, and being REAL. Creating a new story is extremely valuable in the transformation process. It works for changing old beliefs, or bringing spirituality alive within a religious service.

Jesus was a storyteller. He taught through stories. So did Mohammed, Buddha, and other religious leaders. The success of Joseph Campbell's popular TV series on the power of myths emphasizes the strong fascination with myths and storytelling. It seems to be woven into the fabric of human experience. We communicate best by telling our stories. The earliest and oldest pictographs and hieroglyphs tell stories of hunts, of wars, of birth and death. The success of Twelve Step groups is built largely on the sharing of stories in which we find common denominators. So one way to discover the sacred in the secular, to make that sacred body-mind-emotion connection, is to open ourselves to the rich variety of stories available to us.

A friend sent me a delightful book called *The Spirituality of Imperfection* by Ernest Kurtz and Katherine Ketcham. In it, the authors explore a wide array of stories from different sources—religions, philosophy, politics. Explaining why stories are so vital to us, Kurtz says:

Each human being has his or her own story, and every story is unique. But the telling and hearing of those stories takes place in a setting where each participant is conscious of an *identity rooted in limitation.* This foundation of shared weakness invites an attitude that allows differences to be seen as strengths, and therefore as enriching rather than threatening.[1]

So stories help us to become real, with ourselves, and with each other. They also help us connect to the spiritual heritage contained in religious texts. Learning to utilize spiritual insights gained from stories is a powerful move in the God Game. A friend called me recently, needing to reach out. He had been very ill and in great pain. When I asked what he really wanted to do, he avoided telling me directly; instead, he began telling me about what was going on in his life—the steps he'd been trying to take. It became clear that what he really wanted was to die, but he seemed afraid to say it outright. I asked what I could do for him and he said, "Just listen. Just please listen."

When we learn in childhood not to communicate directly, we learn to "sneak" our needs and wants into a story, as my friend did. The God-Box is built of taboos—rules against talking about sex, about feelings, about death. My friend could not tell me directly that he wanted to die, that he felt suicidal. Instead, he told me that he was "forgetting to eat," and despite having lung cancer, had begun smoking again. He was telling me the story of what his pain looked like, leaving it to me to read between the lines. Finally, I got him to talk openly about wanting to die, whether he just wanted out of the pain, or whether there was nothing left in life that gave him any joy. In the end, we were able to talk about it, and he began to discover that there were things he still looked forward to.

What he needed was dialogue, a way of communicating that allowed him to explore his feelings. Yes, he had done the usual things—he had kept a journal, taken walks alone to think things through. He just needed someone to listen while he sorted his thoughts and feelings. I began to wonder how many people end up committing suicide because they cannot talk about wanting to die without fear of judgment. It occurred to me that the Church's condemnation of suicide may force people into that decision because they have no place to tell their story—the *real* story, not the people-pleasing one. Concerned about my friend, I related the situation to a colleague, who startled me by challenging the prevailing views on suicide. "Did you ever think that choosing to die rather than merely endure life could be a powerful move? That it's not cowardly at all, but a courageous stand?" When I reiterated my belief in the sacredness of life, my colleague replied,

"Leo, what is sacred about being in such pain that there is no enjoyment of life? How can we say it's cruel not to put an animal to sleep when it's in great pain, and not imagine that it's just as cruel to force people to live in extreme physical or emotional pain? Isn't that a kind of spiritual abuse?"

While I'm not fully ready to endorse suicide, these dialogues have caused me to look again at myself and my beliefs. As a result, I gained new insights into my own awareness of the many levels of spiritual abuse. At the same time, my relationships with my friend, and with my colleague, were enriched by the level of intimacy achieved by one person's having reached out in pain, and his ultimate willingness to be real. I also wonder what would have happened if I hadn't been able to respond—to read between the lines? We must learn to reveal ourselves more directly, so that we are not relying on other people to figure out what we are really trying to say. We need to learn to tell stories that reveal our REAL selves, not our false fronts.

Changing the story can become a wonderfully creative process. It will allow us to draw on a vast array of materials from many different areas. We can use methods learned in psychology, or metaphysics, or Eastern philosophy or Twelve Step recovery. When we aren't boxed in, we can discover how almost any tool can be used to help build or reclaim spiritual power. Particularly important will be recreating our own special rituals and ceremonies, for these are powerful elements of storytelling. They can reinforce the new stories we are going go tell ourselves about how we are connected to ourselves, and to God.

How do we go about this? One of the most exciting things about playing the God Game is that there aren't any rigid rules; there may be a few tips and guidelines to help you discover your own moves, but since you are no longer a pawn in a spiritual high-stakes contest, rules are not so important. Remember that one definition of "game" is "having a spirit of adventure." Your new partnership with God will be a life-long adventure, with high spots and low spots, to be sure. But hopefully, how you regard those ups and downs will make the difference between spiritual slavery and spiritual empowerment. You will notice that I don't give a lot of hard and fast formulas, exercises or rules for making the moves in the God Game. Instead, as we look at some of the moves made by people in various stages of the process, I hope you will begin to discover how to create your own moves.

Transforming Old Beliefs

As we noted in Chapter Six, cleaning out our God-Box is an ongoing, and often multi-faceted process. We criss-cross through the issues, depending on how they are related, and how critically they impair our lives. Our healing often comes in stages, as we work through the layers of issues. We may begin by dealing with a specific event or issue, such as alcoholism or abuse. Then we begin to work on the long-term effects. This was the case with Annette, who is working through the effects of a repressive Catholic upbringing, and an extramarital affair with a Catholic priest.

I met Annette at a conference where I gave a workshop on healing the wounds of religious abuse. She approached timidly, her fearfulness at odds with her professional dress and demeanor. She looked like an executive: trim, tweed-suited, a striking middle-aged woman. Yet she was shaking like a leaf. "Th-thank you for coming," she stammered. "I-it really helped." Later, in answer to my request for personal stories of clergy abuse, she called my office. Her story was shocking, not so much for what happened to her, but how she felt about it.

She described growing up in "the usual rigid Catholic family with all the good old Catholic guilt and rules." When I met her, she had already been in therapy for a while, and her therapist had helped her see how her childhood set her up to be seduced by her Parish Priest, Father Tom. But she still couldn't move past her self-blame. "I was an adult. I should have known better. It was my fault. I could have said no. He told me it wouldn't be a sin because he was a priest and he was helping me become a better wife. I should have known better than to fall for that," she said bitterly. Reinforcing this guilt was the fact that her husband had divorced her and her church had ostracized her, claiming she had tempted Father Tom. When I met Annette, it had been ten years since the breakup of her marriage. She was working as an executive in a large corporation. Abandoned by family and church, she lived alone, refusing to date, attending Mass in a new church in a new town, but steadfastly avoiding any real contact with the priest. The recent scandals involving clergy abuse had somehow penetrated her staunch self-blame enough to prompt her to come to my workshop. Later, she participated in my annual Conference Cruise.

As I have gotten to know Annette, it is clear that she was set up by religious teachings that constantly emphasized the secondary role of women and the absolute authority of the church. "If a priest says it, it must be true," she believed. Intellectually, she knows that it would never have occurred to her to seduce a priest. "I really didn't think of them as real men who had human feelings. I thought they were above all that." Annette's belief in her own "badness" was responsible for her great fear the night she approached me at the workshop. She believed she was somehow a sex magnet that would "bring down" anyone in clerical garb. Moreover, she had an deeply entrenched core belief that God punishes or rewards people for an almost endless series of minute acts, good or bad. She was absolutely furious at God, and also terrified of her anger, believing she would be punished for being angry at God.

Working with Annette, I asked her if she could remove the belief that God rescues or rewards those who please God by virtue of their perfect behavior, exemplary performance of prayer and ritual, or adherence to whatever set of rules they were taught, what is left to be angry at God about? Is it not then easier to assign accountability to the real perpetrator(s)? This was the question Annette wrestled with over and over as she struggled to rebuild her life following her abuse by Father Tom. She had been raised to believe in the absolute authority and rightness of both the Church and the Clergy. It is upon this rock that the Vatican builds its power. The Church and its leaders, from the Pope to the priests and nuns and lay leaders, are God's representatives on earth. God is perfect; therefore, God's representatives are perfect when they are doing God's business.

Although she didn't like to admit it, Annette carried a deep belief that evils and temptations were created to test her, so if she fell victim to someone else's errors, it meant she had somehow failed a test. "What if," I suggested to Annette, "God created an imperfect world not to test us, but to free us, for in an absolutely perfect world, we have no choices, and therefore, no real spiritual power. Sometimes, we must accept that pain and difficulties are the price we must pay for our spiritual freedom, and yes, sometimes, it seems like a very high and unfair price." She thought about it, and discovered that this idea made her angry at God all over again. "Well, maybe we just have accept that this is how the world is, and with this acceptance, comes a forgiveness of the God we had imagined," I said.

In order to even contemplate the idea of forgiving God, Annette had to reframe her beliefs about God and perfection. This came in stages, the first being acceptance that the church and the clergy were not perfect. "If the Pope, and the nuns and the priests are human, aren't they subject to human error like the rest of us? And if humans were created in God's image, and humans are imperfect, cannot the image of God reflected in creation therefore be imperfect?" I asked Annette. I reminded her that everything we are taught about God has come from people, and is therefore necessarily imperfect. Even if we imagine that God spoke directly to and through certain people, the fact that his information had to pass through the filter of human interpretation and understanding means that we cannot know God absolutely or perfectly.

To help her understand this, I used the analogy of mirrors: we can hone and polish and create the most perfect mirror we can find, and hold it to the sun, but the reflection will never be the sun itself, nor will it contain all of the sun's power. The reflection is subject to flaws, imperfections, distortions, diminishments. Yet we can still refine and retune how we aim our mirror, and how we reflect the sun's energy. This is part of the new story we can begin to tell about God, for it then opens the door to being able to constantly refine and change our understanding of God and thus, how we can relate to God. But Annette still had a hard time moving away from the belief that God despises imperfection and demands that we free ourselves of it.

So we tried another exercise: I asked her if she thought that Jesus was God. Of course, she replied. Did she think Jesus was God incarnate right from the minute he was born? Like many people, Annette hadn't given much thought to the first years of Jesus' life—particularly to his childhood. After all, there's not much information: we know about his birth, then we don't really see what went on until we see him in the temple as a young boy. The next time we see him, he's an adult. I asked Annette to focus on the idea of Jesus as a child. Did he cry when he was wet? Did he have "terrible two's" and tantrums like the rest of us? Did he rebel against his parents as a teenager? Did he fight with his siblings? Surely at some point during his childhood Mary or Joseph had to discipline him; the accounts of his visit to the Temple as a boy indicate they were angry at him for disappearing to talk to the priest when he was supposed to be doing something else. Annette realized she had just assumed that Jesus was an absolutely perfect child. "So you think he came into the world toilet-trained, with all his teeth, and never got sick, or hungry or scared?" I asked. If he didn't do any of those things, then what might have been the purpose of coming into the world as normal humans do, if not to experience the full range *and limitations* of human feelings?

Trying to imagine Jesus as a normal child was still scary for Annette, but she found that she had great sympathy for Mary, whom she believed always knew her child's true identity. "Gosh, poor Mary. Taking care of this little baby, knowing he was the Son of God—*was* God!" Annette said. "I'd have been scared to death."

"What makes you think Mary wasn't?" I asked. "The point is, she took the risk. She had a baby—an illegitimate baby if we want to really stick to Biblical fundamentals, because she wasn't legally married. She asked her fiance to raise the child as his own. Don't you think that was pretty scary?"

This conversation proved to be the pivotal point in Annette's being able to come to terms with the presence of imperfection in the world. If, as she believed, God had chosen to come into the world and live as humans do, then yes, at some point in those 33 years, God in the person of Jesus just might have screwed up once or twice. Made Joseph mad. Made Mary tear her hair in frustration. Made them proud. Made them sad. Just like any other child. Annette did a whole series of drawings and dialogues about Jesus as a child, and through these, slowly began to turn around her belief that God requires absolute perfection, and therefore, that those who serve God must be perfect. She allowed herself to read the *Bible* totally on her own, without the catechisms, doctrines and rituals that enshrouded it. She started looking for instances in which Jesus expressed human feelings—particularly those that she had been taught were "bad." She saw him get angry and lonely, feel victimized and abandoned, fearful and resistant. She saw him rebel against authority.

In short, she saw Jesus doing many of the things she had been taught not to do. She began to see not the plaster saints—the crucified, bleeding Lord and saintly Virgin, but human people manifesting real spiritual power in the very humanness of their actions. She realized that she had never believed that Jesus, Mary or Joseph had any choice about what was happening, and saw how the Church had glossed this over with a whole lot of magical wonders to make that OK. She began to tell herself a new story about of the life of Christ—one in which all the players were not perfect puppets, but instead could have chosen at any time not to play. In her revised story, Jesus saves us by showing us how to live with and respond to, imperfection, rather than merely buying time for us via his crucifixion until we "get perfect."

As her understanding and acceptance of the presence of imperfection grew, so did her trust, first in herself, and then in other people, especially men. When we first met, she had been bitterly distrustful not only of me, because I am a priest (guilt by association), but of nearly everyone. Once she recognized that her distrust grew out of her expectation that "good" people were also "perfect" people, she began to discover that her world was actually filled with very good people whom she could trust—not because they were perfect, but because they were willing to acknowledge when they made mistakes and most of all, seemed not to mind when she made them.

Today, Annette continues to use this process of challenging and questioning not only of religious authority, but of authority in general. She was very pleased to tell me about an incident at work in which another vice president insisted a project had been fully completed. Although everyone wanted to push on to end the meeting, Annette persisted in questioning: information in his report seemed rather sketchy in one or two areas; was it possible that those particular parts had not been completed? Further questioning and investigation proved that indeed, she was correct, and some vital details had been overlooked, that might have had disastrous results later on. Annette feared she would be ostracized by her colleagues, as she had been by her congregation. To her surprise, they treated her with renewed respect and open approval. Even more surprising to her, she understood that the other vice president's brief avoidance of her was not condemnation of her, but his own embarrassment. The more Annette takes steps like this, the closer she comes to accepting that the feeling of pride and excitement she feels inside just might be God giving her a big "thumbs up" of approval.

The process I went through with Annette is typical of how transforming old beliefs works. It's kind of like untangling a big knot. Her core beliefs that God demands perfection and punishes imperfection were all snarled up with her belief in the absolute authority and infallibility of the clergy and the Church. Then there was the distrust that grew out of her painful experiences with Father Tom. No matter what your religion or philosophy, you can use a similar process of challenge, questions and exploration to move away from disempowering beliefs. In this way, you begin to write a new story about who you are, who God is, and the kind of relationship you can have.

WRITING A NEW SCRIPT

The beliefs and messages we have accumulated into our God-Box become the script we follow throughout our lives. As I discussed earlier, what we believe about God, we become. Because these messages and beliefs determine how we will respond in almost any situation, even when we "improvise" a little bit, and think we've actually written a new script, we aren't able to move very far from the confines of our God-Box. Thus, many of our ongoing moves involve replacing what is in our God-Box with a whole new batch of scripts. This is the process I began with Annette. In learning how to question and dialogue, she was actually learning how to start writing a new set of scripts that offered more spiritual freedom.

Understanding the value of being able to move out of the confines of one set of beliefs and "write your own script" opens the door to immense spiritual power. In *As Above, So Below*, Ronald Miller explores how aspects of shamanism and Native American spirituality can help people begin to discover a new connectedness to themselves and the world. He quotes the late Native American teacher Sun Bear, who said:

> The path of power is different for every individual . . . It is why you are here. When I speak of power, I mean a way of working and using all your energy—including your spiritual energy—in a direction that allows you to become a whole person, capable of fulfilling whatever vision the Creator gives to you. Finding your path of power is not always easy. For me to do it, I had to tear up both the white man's and the Indian's scripts for life. If you wish to walk the path of power, you must do the same.[2]

I found a powerful illustration of how this works in the film, *Searching For Bobby Fischer*, which is another story of courage and empowerment. In it, young chess prodigy Josh Waitkin is torn between two mentors: a street-wise black man who teaches him how to play speed chess in a Greenwich Village park, and the elitist chess master who is constantly searching for the next Bobby Fischer, one of the world's greatest chess players. The rules and styles of chess practiced by his two teachers are almost opposite: the aggressive, lightning-quick moves of speed chess, and the slow, cerebral, almost ritualized formal chess that is regulated by thousands of rules and moves. As the story unfolds, it is clear that the child has an innate understanding and love of the game; he becomes equally adept at both disciplines. As he moves higher in the rankings of tournament competitions, the conflict between his teachers grows more intense. When he is forbidden to play with his teacher from the park, he loses his love of the game—we see the light go out. Ultimately, he goes back to the park to play the way he loves, and, in the final championship game, blends the teachings of both his mentors. This is empowerment: not yielding to one or the other, but drawing on the best of both and trusting his own innate instincts. Like Sun Bear, he had to tear up the "scripts" both of his mentors wrote for him and make his own moves.

In the God-Game, our spiritual moves come from our ability to choose, from the knowledge within ourselves that we can draw on the entire library of religion, philosophy, and theology to build the foundation of our relationship with God. When we are not boxed in by one set of teachings that often serves to divide us, we are free to discover commonalities in all faiths that can enrich and enlighten us. Some people may choose to retain a literal, fundamentalist belief system. If this is the framework that works for them, that is fine, so long as they don't insist that I am wrong or evil if I choose a different path. Growing up in our relationship with God means that we get to choose how we will involve God in our lives, instead of being told what to do and when to do it and what will happen if we don't, as if we were still little children. This is the key to spiritual empowerment. As a priest, I no longer dictate to people what they must believe and which rituals they must follow to express that belief. Today, I am a priest who tries to show people how to dialogue with God, how to discover the many ways in which we can experience God, and how to discover their own inner wisdom.

Creating a "new story" sometimes involves just a slight change in wording, as Anna did by merely substituting "friend" for "wretch" in that disempowering line from the hymn "Amazing Grace." Other times, as we saw in the reworking of Psalm 23, we need to do an extensive overhaul, or we will end up with our same old spiritual "dirty laundry" repackaged in a new suitcase. It may look nice until we have to open it up and expose the same old moldy, smelly insides of the God-Box.

What we can be is virtually limitless, within the boundaries of our human existence. When we are not bound by the God-Box, when we feel free to make our own moves, we can truly experience the mystery of the universe—the sacred in the secular. When we find God everywhere in the world—in a movie, in a casual conversation between friends—even on the evening news, we discover we can tap into our spiritual power at almost any time or any place.

I heard one of the most awesome examples of spiritual empowerment on the evening news. A man was cutting down a tree when it suddenly fell on him, breaking his leg and pinning him to the ground. As he struggled to free himself, he realized he was in mortal danger. He was deep into the woods; no one knew where he was. Worse, he was bleeding badly from the wounded leg. He tried to dig his leg out from under the tree and could not. Finally, he realized that he would die out there if he didn't do something. Fortunately, he was able to reach his pocketknife and, slowly, painfully, cut through the skin, muscle and tendons around the broken bone until he amputated his leg. Then he dragged himself to his truck and drove to the nearest farmhouse. No one was home. He had to drive further on before finding help. Sure, he could have stayed under that tree and prayed for God to send rescuers. Instead, he called on his own spiritual power: clear-headedness and ability to reason; courage, and a will to live that made him willing to endure the pain of what he had to do.

Cutting off his leg was the prayer, a sacrifice in its most elemental form and a supreme act of faith. Like the Israelites in the story of the Exodus, who fearfully walked into the midst of the parted waters of the Red Sea, this man created his own miracle, and in the process, became co-creator of his life. This is genuine spiritual empowerment, a true partnership with God and the beauty and terror of the world around us. He literally walked with God through unimaginable pain in order to save his own life.

To me, this is also an example of experiencing the awesome mystery of God, not in some theatrical Cecil B. DeMille-type spectacle, but in the incredible workings of the human spirit. The mystery and majesty of God is that we were created in such intricate fashion. The way our bodies, minds and emotions work together to create our spiritual energy is astounding. Taking God and spirituality "out of the ethers" and "earthing" it by increasing our awareness of God's presence in our world connects us to the mystery, allows us to participate in it with God. We cease to become just spectators, and become part of the action. The more we can increase our ability to respond to what God has placed in this world, the more we are able to experience and appreciate the mystery of God.

Increasing Our Response-Ability

Experiencing God involves a connectedness to ourselves, mentally, emotionally and physically. Through this connection, we are able to deepen our connection to others. When we are able to move out of one set script, we can appreciate and experience "The Way" demonstrated not just by Jesus, but by so many great spiritual leaders and teachers in all cultures and walks of life. Writing a new story for ourselves helps us discover the sacred in the secular that reveals God at work in so many diverse places—not only in the traditional religious scriptures, but in the words of ordinary people who challenge us to connect with our world. Yet in that diversity, we can find a shared connection. Look at the similarities between Jesus's instructions to his disciples in *Matthew 25: 35-45*, and a speech given in 1855 by the Duwamish Indian Chief Seattle to Governor Stevens of Washington Territory:

MATTHEW 25

For I was hungry, and you gave me no food; thirsty, and you gave me no drink; I was a stranger, and you did not welcome me. . . . Truly, I say to you, as you did it not to the least of these, you did it not to me.

CHIEF SEATTLE

All things are bound together.
All things connect.
What happens to the Earth
happens to the children of the Earth.
Man has not woven the web of life.
He is but one thread.
Whatever he does to the web
he does to himself. [3]

Two holy men, nearly two thousand years apart, make the common plea for us to connect, to be mindful of how our actions affect others, and through the way we affect others, we affect our relationship with God. What makes them holy is not so much who they were, but how we respond to their core spiritual message. For if we do not respond, if we do not connect what they say to how we live our lives, then we miss discovering their sacredness.

Increasing our inner connectedness, our "Response-Ability" that lets us find our spiritual power in many places and situations takes time, and practice. Like playing a musical instrument, or excelling in a sport, we have to practice our spiritual power in order to strengthen and grow in it. As we saw in Chapter Six, this often involves befriending and embracing your "Shadow" sides. Remember, our "Shadow" or "dark" sides are those parts of ourselves we repressed, rejected or abandoned as a result of the messages we received in childhood from our families, our religions and/or our society. If we can rewrite the story we tell about ourselves, then we can include many of these allegedly "bad" parts: our feelings, our freedom to evaluate and choose, and of course, our sexuality.

Sometimes, our "Shadow" sides include things like addictions, compulsions, judgmentalism, negativity, criminal behavior or hateful attitudes. But often, our Dark Side is less sinister. For instance, mine is named, "Not Good Enough." I've described how that part of me developed, from the messages I got in my childhood. Many of you may have had similar experiences. When your life is set out for you in a script titled "Not Good Enough," it will be almost impossible to love or accept all of yourself. In *Your Child's Self Esteem*, Dorothy Corkhill Briggs wrote this moving account of what happens when you feel you are never enough:

> A fifteen-year-old boy, living with parents whose standards were rigid, authoritarian and in no way appropriate to his nature, said, "I'm completely resigned. There's nothing I can do about my parents. I can't get them to change, so I'm going to have to change. Anything I feel or want to be . . . well, it just means trouble. . . . I guess I died when I was born. The way I really am couldn't please my family or anybody. How do you get rid of what you are?"[4]

This boy's cry of pain could very well have come from young Leo Booth, although I could never have come close to articulating it so well at that age. By then, I'd already disconnected from my feelings in order to avoid this boy's despair and resignation, that sense of "having died before I was born." Needing to substitute something for feelings, I turned to religion and later, to alcohol. In recovery, I have allowed the young Leo who felt fearful and stifled to dream, to reach out, to create. I have turned my rebellious love of a good challenge towards helping others discover their spiritual creative power.

Yet I find that my spiritual restlessness remains with me. Not surprisingly, the name of this restlessness is "Not good enough." When my goals, dreams and desires seem to dance tantalizingly out of my grasp, I push myself harder. Unfortunately, I also push others around me just as hard. After a particularly difficult staff meeting one day, one of my staff said to me, "You know Leo, I don't know why I bother. Nothing we do is ever good enough. You never seem to acknowledge what we've accomplished here. You're always focusing on what we *don't* have."

My God, how those words hurt. That I, who strive to empower people and help them discover their own positive specialness, could actually reinforce a sense of helplessness and despair was shocking. But yet, when I looked at it, I discovered it was true. It became another "Harry Moment,"—one of those transformative "Stop! Look! Change!" times. In seeking to move myself out of helplessness into empowerment, I lost sight of an important Spiritual Value: Harmony and Balance. Pursuing my choices and options, I had forgotten to stand still long enough to appreciate what I and my staff do as a team. My staff members have taught themselves to use computers and do incredibly creative things with limited knowledge and equipment; they constantly stretch and challenge themselves. And I truly thought I was helping them meet those challenges by spurring them on. I'd excused my behavior by insisting that nothing would get done if we didn't constantly push ourselves. I thought I was "giving my prayers feet." But it was finally brought home to me that I had not changed the language I was using. I was still using pieces of that old script. And not being fully present to the moment—not "stopping to smell the roses"—kept me from hearing my words and my tone of voice. It stopped me from responding in the way that I wanted to respond.

This was especially difficult to acknowledge because so many of the calls and letters I get from people describe feelings of "Not Good Enough," and the little boy inside me always related so deeply to such stories. For a while, my old Shadow self took over and I wallowed in some good old victimized righteous indignation. But that part of me is not as strong as it once was. Yes, it pops out, as I've described, but then the empowered Leo returns to confront the crisis head-on. I had some long chats with myself about balance and about how to start rewriting those parts of the old shaming script that can be so reflexive.

My first step was to acknowledge not just that my staff member was right on, but to also applaud the courage and spiritual power that confronting me revealed. Then I looked at what "Not Good Enough" had been doing to me: keeping me on the road for long hours, racking my brains about how to keep my small business afloat in these changing times. I realized I'd been neglecting myself physically, so I began working out regularly. I saw that my emotional needs were also being slighted, so I made sure to include fun things in my schedule—a movie, a book, dinner out with a friend. And I began to make a conscious effort to remind myself of all that I have done when "Not Good Enough" starts whispering in my ear so that I don't abuse myself or others around me.

This is the process I use of reframing, rewriting my scripts to increase my "Response-Ability." As I said in Chapter Six, we don't clean out the God-Box all at once. Creating an adult relationship with God is an ongoing process of ups and downs, balance and imbalance. It is a process of refining, going back, working on the basics some more, then moving to a different level. It's the process artists and musicians use to hone their craft—practicing, practicing the very simple things, then adding more complicated techniques and skills. I'm always amazed to hear that the great classical musicians like Placido Domingo or Itzhak Perlman still practice each day. My confrontation with my staff reminded me I'd let my "practicing" slip.

Rituals as a Means of Practicing Our Moves
I often hear people talking about "spiritual practice." Usually, they are referring to meditation, prayer, or the use of affirmations and rituals. All of these can be effective means of helping us write new stories and "practicing" our moves. But these are not the only means of spiritual practice. As I described above, our practice involves remaining aware of what we are doing, and being willing to recognize when we have let some of our spiritual garbage pollute our efforts.

There are many ways to practice. My staff member was "practicing" when she confronted me about "Not Good Enough." But prior to that, she had also undergone many seminars and workshops on dealing with her own anger and healthy expression of feelings. These were vital parts of her spiritual practice. Similarly, my friend Anna recently had to tell a close friend who was dumping a lot of venomous rage and frustration on her to either find an appropriate container for that rage or they'd have to cancel dinner plans. For Anna, who usually cowers and submits to others' anger, this was an incredibly powerful move. But again, she didn't just jump out and make it. She had to practice—work her way to that point—over a length of time, and utilizing tools gained from therapy, support groups, affirmations, and earlier moves.

This is important for Anna, who is a survivor of ritualized abuse while in nursery school. Working through that process has been arduous for Anna. So many times, she runs out of hope and just wants to die. In those times, she says, "God is so very far away." To help her through those times, her therapist has encouraged her to create her own rituals and celebrations as part of her healing process. Anna's moves in the God-Game involve her willingness to move out of trauma, and create new ways in which to use ritual as a means of relating to God. To do this, she has empowered herself to set boundaries about what is safe, and although her friends often don't understand why she won't go to this church or that one, she remains firm. She is currently exploring Native American teachings, but chooses not to attend the local Native American church. "I don't want to make a religion of anything," she says. "The minute there's a religion and a set of beliefs and practices stuck to something, it gets boxed in." Having been literally boxed up as a toddler during her ritual abuse, Anna rebels against the confinements of any specific religion, preferring to explore and use whatever spiritual practices feel safe and nurturing.

Anna calls her rituals "celebrations" so that she doesn't feel obligated to perform them daily. I have met many recovering Catholics who, having been conditioned to the many rituals—the prayers, the rosary beads, the incense—of the Catholic church, similarly seek healthy ways to use rituals in their lives. Some make a practice of talking to God during a morning walk. Others read daily meditation books at a special time set aside in the day. Some people use journal writing as their means of talking with God. The point is that God can be found anywhere we remember to involve God.

The reason that healthy rituals are important is that they can become a means to "earthing" an adult relationship with God—making it alive and tangible. They connect us to the mystery of God. The childish relationship with God is very passive. The prayers, rituals, and doctrines reinforce the passivity, by constantly telling us what God will do for us or to us. They do not call on us to act. Prayer is an action—a verb. In the adult relationship with God, each choice becomes a prayer, a part of the dialogue with God. Seeking therapy, learning new ways to communicate, seeking or accepting change, all become our celebrations, the rituals of co-creatorship. Each time we connect to God's energy becomes a small celebration of our partnership with God.

The key to creating any healthy ritual or ceremony is that it should always seek to unite us mentally, emotionally, or physically so that we can increase our spiritual responsiveness. It can be designed to help us accept or reinforce some powerful aspect of ourselves, or as a means of reframing—writing our new scripts. There are many workbooks and guide books for creating your own meditations, writing your own affirmations and developing your own rituals. A friend's therapist suggested that when she puts lotion on after a shower, she should take time to really *feel* what she is doing: nurturing and loving herself, getting to know her body. This is especially good for people who have body image problems. In her book *Fire In the Soul,* Joan Borysenko shares the following guidelines for a "walking meditation" that reminds her to open herself to awareness of the smells, textures and colors around her. It helps her notice her body—how it feels to touch the earth, the rhythms of her walking, and of her breath. The meditation, by Vietnamese Buddhist monk Thich Nhat Hanh, ends with this description of the benefits that "mindful walking" could bring:

> The practice of walking meditation opens your eyes to wonders in the universe. It turns samsara (the world of illusions) into Pure Land (heaven). It lets sorrow and worry fall away, and brings peace. But walking meditation also helps us to see the pain, anguish and suffering. When we are aware, we can see clearly what is happening in life . . . Scented paths across the rice fields, shady bamboo-lined dirt roads, parks covered with dark-colored dry leaves—these are your paths for walking meditation; please enjoy them. They should not lead you to forgetfulness so that you cannot see the real dramas of the world. Then every path, every street—from the back alleys of Beirut to the roads of Vietnam where mines still explode and take the lives of children and farmers—every path in the world is your walking meditation path. Once you are awake, you will not hesitate to enter these paths . . . You will suffer, but your pain will not come from your own worries and fears. You will suffer because of your kinship with all beings, because you have the compassion of an awakened being . . . [5]

Awakening to her feelings, in all the myriad ways in which they express themselves, is how Marcella learned to find God. In the opening to Chapter Four, she wrote movingly of how she had looked in so many places, and could not find God. The harder she searched for God, the angrier Marcella got that God was so elusive, and the more she retreated from the world that only reminded her painfully of God's absence. I asked Marcella, "If you had found God, what would it have felt like?" She described a variety of emotions: awe, exhilaration, peace, and serenity. Had she never in her whole life felt any of those feelings? What happened to produce them? What kept her from feeling God's presence? As I suspected, when it came down to it, Marcella had spent all those years searching, with no real notion of what she was seeking, except that she somehow expected to feel removed, transported, uplifted, taken away, *carried.*

I suggested to Marcella that she begin to take notice of all the places she could find God every day. She kept little notebooks with her at all times so that she could jot down places where she found God throughout the day. Marcella had spent most of her life in a foggy blur. She had not lived her life, but merely endured it, mostly by disconnecting herself from her feelings. At first, her notebooks were full of things like, "I smelled the roses on my walk today ... I watched the children in the park and heard their laughter ... I saw a homeless man help an old woman across the street." Gradually, she grew more in touch with her feelings. She began to notice how her body reacted to stress: "No wonder my arthritis is kicking up. I had my hands clenched all morning. Couldn't think why. Then I realized, it's Mother's birthday. I used to get all tense, hoping she would like the gift I bought her." In this manner, Marcella began connecting her mental, emotional, and physical responses to understand what was going on within her, and therefore change her responses to the world. Before making this connection, she would feel victimized and helpless, fearing she was going to be incapacitated by arthritis. Now she sees how her emotional reactions actually contribute to some of her physical ailments.

As she began getting in touch with painful childhood memories—memories of frightening, lonely times when she tried to find God—she would imagine her newfound adult self talking to the child she had been, showing her where God was, showing her that God had been there all along.

KEEPING YOUR MOVES ALIVE

One of the most exciting and challenging parts of playing the God Game is to continue to use the moves we make to help make other moves. The purpose of "writing new scripts" is to take us on a more powerful road. When we learn to connect the elements of spiritual empowerment wherever they are found—in our daily lives, the evening news, our religious and inspirational texts, or the trauma of our own pain—we discover that we have a vast storehouse of scripts we can draw on to guide our moves.

One of the best examples of how our small, daily moves can prepare us for the "big" moves comes in the biblical story of David and Goliath. The traditional interpretation of this story is that, by invoking the name of the God of Israel as he challenged Goliath, David magically received God's power and so was able to bring down the Philistine warrior. I have often heard it said that God directed David's aim—that God did it, not David. But I think this story is actually a vivid example of how we draw on our small moves to make other moves and, in so doing, strengthen our creative partnership with God.

First, David took responsibility—he took action. He had been sent to the battle site to bring food to his brothers. He was appalled at the sight of all these mighty soldiers being cowed by one man. When they told him he was a mere shepherd and not trained in warfare, David pointed out that he was trained in warfare against bigger, stronger enemies. After all, he was a shepherd who had to fight off bears and wolves every day. All he had to do was imagine that Goliath was just another big bear threatening his flock.

The soldiers wanted to load David down with armor and weapons, but he wasn't comfortable with that. He used his own weapons: five smooth stones. God didn't pick the stones; David did, drawing on the skills and instincts honed by days in the fields. When a shepherd is up against a hungry bear, every shot must count, and David certainly knew how to do that. He had spent hours and hours practicing in the fields with his slingshot, learning how to spot the best stones, strengthening his coordination and speed. These were his "little moves"—the daily moves he needed to make in order to be a good shepherd. In choosing to use the tools and skills he knew best, David drew on these little moves to create his "big move" against Goliath. In drawing on his daily partnership with God, he co-created his win. If David had garbed himself in the traditional armor rather than use the skills he knew he possessed, would he have succeeded? Doubtful. As I see it, the armor is a metaphor for the traditional religious teachings that were not working. David set those aside to look within himself for the strength and skills to accomplish his mission.

In this story, we can see not a magical "fix" but the empowerment to discover and use our own special gifts. In a childish relationship with God, David would have had no choice but to go up against Goliath wearing armor that was not suitable for him. In an adult partnership with God, he was free to choose how he would tackle the problem. "Rewriting the script" about what this story means is one move we make. In doing so, we discover some ideas about how to keep our moves alive so that we can draw on them when we need them.

We can't just stay still in our creative moments. We need to continue to use these moments as David did. I met a modern-day David, a Vietnam veteran named Don who shared with me a remarkable story of how he has come to terms with the pain of war. After attending my workshop, he suddenly realized that much of his pain came from conflicts between what he heard in his religious upbringing and the senselessness of war. The religious messages of his childhood made no sense in the context of his adulthood, and he has rightly, I think, identified this conflict as one of the unresolved core issues that keep Vietnam veterans, and all war vets, in pain and turmoil.

He wrote to me that his rigid, black-and-white religious upbringing at first made him a "natural" military man. Putting all your faith in God and not questioning an external figure made it easy for him to believe that God had given divine orders to the United States government leaders. But Don discovered that this black-and-white thinking had its flip side: "When I realized I was involved in a cauldron of evil, then where is God's place in this? Black-and-white world/black-and-white religious upbringing then flips the other way: God must be all bad! God was AWOL! (Absent Without Leave)"

Don believed that it was his fault, that if he had better faith, the war would never have been, or it would have been won. His torment led him into addiction and deeper torment. In recovery he realized he needed to work through three emotional pains: the pain of betrayal, the pain with no meaning, and the pain of not being understood. He began writing to help sort through the pain and confusion. One thing he did to help heal the pain was to find the common bond between himself and the Vietnamese soldiers he fought. Where religious and political dogma sought to create difference and hate, he actively sought union, to recognize that the men, women, and children labeled "enemy" had the same feelings, the same fears, and the same hopes. He used his poetry and writing to work through his bitterness and confusion, and to help him identify and begin to address his issues.

But he is not content to stop there. Today, he not only works with other United States veterans, he has also created an outreach program for Soviet and Afghanistan veterans who share problems similar to those of American and Vietnamese soldiers. One Soviet soldier told him, "You understand me better than anyone in my own country." Having learned how to relate to and embrace his enemy, he is now sharing his moves with others.

Don is an excellent example of how we keep our "moments" alive, and how we recognize other moments that come our way. He writes to me that he has finally begun to move through the pain and rage of believing that God was AWOL. In discovering the bonds he shares with others, he has discovered that God was there all along. He understands that what he *was taught* about God made no sense. In Vietnam, he had a conversation with a chaplain about how he could possibly not be punished for breaking the commandment not to kill. The chaplain told him, "If a person had hate in his heart when he killed, it was murder; if he killed without hate, he was innocent." Recalling this bizarre conversation, Don wondered how this man thought it was possible to kill without hate, for hate is the trigger. In a moment of bitterness, he mused that if he were God looking at the wounding done in his name, he would be tempted to destroy the whole world and start over. Don ended this particular essay with the thought:

> But it is Sunday morning and I am not God. I am a man that walks in the leaves, thinks of what Sunday morning could be, and how we could love each other. What if an adult from our culture, a man that grew up among us, tried to teach us like Christ did? He would have a short time before death or life in a nut house.

I hope Don will discover that he *is* that man who is "teaching like Christ did." I hope he will find that although he is not God, he has already reached and activated God Within him. In the process of his own healing and the way he shares his "moment" with others, he has reclaimed his spiritual power and is actively using it. Like the biblical David, he has drawn on his little moves. The steps he took to heal his own pain are like the stones David learned to throw to drive away ferocious beasts. Having learned how to "find his stones," Don then shared this skill with others like him. To work with Russian soldiers in the days before Communism collapsed was very much like tackling Goliath, yet Don knew he had skills that all the politicians and so-called experts in both countries did not. What a marvelous example of connecting, first within himself, and then to the world around him! And in that connection, he discovered the transforming power of making our spiritual moves. Not only was he able to transform himself, but that transformation then helped transform others. Don drew on his own healing to contribute, in a very real way, to healing global spiritual wounds.

Like Don, my ongoing moves involve sharing the small moves I've made with others. I hope you will also discover that, like David, Don, and the others you've met here, you have been making very vital and powerful spiritual moves. I hope you have gained a new understanding of spirituality that now allows you not only to recognize and appreciate your moves, but to keep them going to discover a new understanding of how religion can become spiritually alive. With a new understanding of spirituality and the recognition of how you can bring the Spiritual Values of Truth, Love, Change, and Harmony in your life, you can create a rich and powerful partnership with God.

When you join with God as partners in the adventurous circle of life, there is no right or wrong way to play, no beginning or end to the game. Each of us plays the God Game differently because it's our life, our adventure. We may invite others into the game or share in their own playing of the God Game. We are always playing—when we are still and when we are moving. By now I hope you know that you've been playing the game with me all through this book. With every response, you've made a move. Even though we do not know each other, we have connected. You are transformed. I am transformed. That is how the God Game works.

The excitement of the God Game is the discovery, the journey. There will be joyous times when you dance with God in the circle, quiet times in which you sit and rest, frightening times in which you feel confused and disconnected, and vibrant times when you pulse with positive, creative spiritual power. No matter where you are in the game, God is with you, your partner in every move you make. This is the knowledge that transforms your relationship with God from passive pawn to powerful player: the awareness that God is, and has always been, active and involved in your life and your world.

Welcome to the God Game. It's your move!

NOTES

1. "Each human being has his or her own story . . . " Kurtz, Ernest and Ketcham, Katherine. *The Spirituality of Imperfection: Modern Wisdom From Classic Stories.* (New York: Bantam Books, 1992). p. 204.

2. "The path of power . . . " Miller, Ronald, ed. *As Above, So Below.* (Los Angeles: Jeremy P. Tarcher, Inc. 1992). p. 73.

3. "All things are bound together . . . " Chief Seattle. *How Can One Sell The Air: A Manifesto For The Earth.* Excerpts from 1985 speech to Governor Stevens. (Summertown, TN: Book Publishing Company, 1980).

4. "A fifteen-year-old boy . . . " Briggs, Dorothy Corkhille. *Your Child's Self-Esteem.* (Garden City, New York: Doubleday and Company, 1970). p. 50.

5. "In her book *Fire In the Soul,* . . . " Borysenko, Joan. *Fire In the Soul: A New Psychology of Spiritual Optimism.* (New York: Warner Books, 1993). pp. 192-194.

BIBLIOGRAPHY

"Sins of the Father" *People.* July 2, 1992.

Abrams, Jeremiah and Zweig, Connie, eds. *Meeting the Shadow: The Hidden Power of the Dark Side of Human Nature.* Los Angeles: Jeremy P. Tarcher, Inc., 1992.

Armstrong, Karen. *A History of God: The 4,000-Year Quest of Judaism, Christianity and Islam.* New York: Alfred A. Knopf, 1993.

Bander, Richard and Grinder, John. *Reframing: Neuro-Linguistic Programming and the Transformation of Meaning.* Moab, Utah: Real People Press, 1982.

Booth, Father Leo. *Spirituality and Recovery: A Guide to Positive Living.* Deerfield Beach, FL: Health Communications, 1985.

Booth, Father Leo. *Meditations For Compulsive People.* Unpublished manuscript.

Borysenko, Joan. *Guilt Is the Teacher, Love Is the Lesson.* New York: Warner Books, 1990.

Borysenko, Joan. *Fire In the Soul: A New Psychology of Spiritual Optimism.* New York: Warner Books, 1993.

Briggs, Dorothy Corkhille. *Your Child's Self-Esteem.* Garden City, New York: Doubleday and Company, 1970.

Erikson, Erik. *Childhood and Society.* New York: W.W. Norton, 1964.

Fortune, Marie M. *Is Nothing Sacred? The Story of a Pastor, the Women He Sexually Abused, and the Congregation He Nearly Destroyed.* San Francisco: HarperCollins, 1989.

Hample, Stuart and Marshall, Eric. *Children's Letters To God.* New York: Workman Publishing, 1991.

Houston, Jean. *The Search For the Beloved: Journeys in Mythology and Sacred Psychology.* Los Angeles: Jeremy P. Tarcher, Inc., 1987.

Hudson, Pamela. *Ritual Child Abuse: Discovery, Diagnosis and Treatment.* Saratoga, CA: R & E Publishers, 1991.

Josephs, Jai. *"I Love Myself the Way I Am."* St. Mary, Kentucky: Living Love Publications.

Kurtz, Ernest and Ketcham, Katherine. *The Spirituality of Imperfection: Modern Wisdom From Classic Stories.* New York: Bantam Books, 1992.

Larsen, Earnie and Prague, Jane. *Recovering Catholics.* San Francisco: HarperCollins, 1992.

Meadows, Kenneth. *Earth Medicine: A Shamanic Way to Self-Discovery.* Longmead, England: Element Books, 1989.

Melville, Arthur. *With Eyes To See: A Journey From Religion to Spirituality.* Walpole, NH: Stillpoint Publishing, 1992.

Miller, Ronald, ed. *As Above, So Below.* Los Angeles: Jeremy P. Tarcher, Inc., 1992.

Miller, Alice. *For Your Own Good.* New York: The Noonday Press, 1990.

Moore, Thomas. *Care of the Soul: A Guide For Cultivating Depth and Sacredness in Everyday Life.* New York: HarperCollins Publishers, 1992.

White, William, *Arkansas Gazette.*

Williams, Margery. *The Velveteen Rabbit.* New York: Avon Books, 1985.

Williamson, Marianne. *A Return to Love.* New York: HarperCollins, 1992.

Ywahoo, Dhyani. *Voices of Our Ancestors: Cherokee Teachings from the Wisdom Fire.* Boston: Shambhala Publications, Inc., 1987.

ADDITIONAL RESOURCES

Addiction and Grace: Love and Spirituality in the Healing of Addictions. Gerald G. May, M.D. HarperCollins, 1988.

Becoming Whole Again: Help for Women Survivors of Childhood Sexual Abuse. Dr. Vera Gallegher. TAB Books, 1991.

Broken Boys, Mending Men: Recovery From Childhood Sexual Abuse. Stephen D. Grubman-Black. TAB Books, 1990.

But She Said: Feminist Practices of Biblical Interpretation. Elizabeth Schussler Fiorenza. Beacon Press, 1992.

Creating Love: The Next Great Stage of Love. John Bradshaw. Bantam Books, 1992.

Dirt, Greed and Sex: Sexual Ethics in the New Testament and Their Implications For Today. L. William Countryman. Fortress Press, 1990.

The Drama of the Gifted Child: The Search For the True Self. Alice Miller. Basic Books, 1981.

Excess Baggage: Getting Out of Your Own Way. Judith Sills, Ph.D. Penguin Books, 1993.

The Inner Child Workbook: What to Do With Your Past When It Just Won't Go Away. Cathryn L. Taylor. Jeremy P. Tarcher, Inc., 1991.

Lead Us Not Into Temptation: Catholic Priests and the Sexual Abuse of Children. Jason Berry. Doubleday Press, 1992.

Lost and Found Along the Way: The Co-Dependent Christian. Ted Zawistowski. Fairway Press, 1992.

A Modern Priest Looks At His Outdated Church. James Kavenaugh. Steven J. Nash Publishing, 1992.

Rescuing the Bible From Fundamentalism: A Bishop Rethinks the Meaning of Scripture. John Shelby Spong. HarperCollins, 1991.

The Road Less Traveled: A New Psychology of Love, Traditional Values and Spiritual Growth. M. Scott Peck, M.D. Simon and Schuster, Inc., 1978.

Say Yes To Life: 365 Daily Meditations. Father Leo Booth. Health Communications, 1988.

"Sustaining the Spirit" *Open Hands* Volume 1, Number 4, Spring, 1992. (An excellent example of how to write an empowering new service.)

WHEN GOD BECOMES A DRUG: Breaking the Chains of Religious Addiction and Abuse. Father Leo Booth. Jeremy P. Tarcher, Inc., 1992.

For a catalog of Father Leo Booth's books, audios and videos, call Spiritual Concepts at (800) 284-2804.

You may write to Father Leo care of:

Spiritual Concepts
2700 St. Louis Avenue
Long Beach, California 90806

ABOUT THE AUTHOR

Dynamic and funny, provocative and insightful, Father Leo Booth is a priest cut from a decidedly different cloth. Although he remains active as a Parish Priest within the Episcopal Church, he insists that religion is not the sole door to spirituality. In fact, he says that spirituality is the soul of religion, and you do not need to be religious in order to be spiritual.

Born in England, his childhood was scarred by the violent arguments between his Catholic father and Anglican (Episcopal) mother. Later, he would realize that becoming a priest was one way to stop the religious arguments. He became one of the youngest rectors in England, and also became an alcoholic. A drunk driving accident in 1977 became the transformative moment that led to his becoming an internationally acclaimed author, lecturer, and spiritual motivator. Since that time, he has dedicated himself to helping people discover their spiritual power and create a mature partnership with God that allows for choice, responsibility, and power.

A certified addictions and eating disorders counselor, he has served as a spiritual consultant to many treatment programs, hospitals, and organizations throughout the country and even Asia and the Philippines. He has developed a dramatic new spiritual model based on connecting, Body, Mind, and Emotions, and teaches this program to hospitals, associations, therapists, clergy, and other organizations. His emphasis on spirituality being different from religion, and the issues creating spiritual abuse attract people from all walks of life who are seeking a healthy spirituality and a more positive, creative relationship with God.

TO OUR READERS

As publishers we seek to live in ways that lighten our human load on the Earth's natural systems and our global environment.

This book is printed on chlorine-free recycled paper (minimum 10% post consumer waste) to save trees and to encourage pulp and paper companies to convert to production processes that do not create highly toxic wastes such as dioxin and other organochlorines.

The Environmental Protection Agency and many other public health agencies have found that dioxin (a by-product created when wood pulp is chlorine bleached) poses a cancer risk to humans and can have harmful effects on immune and reproductive systems of individuals.

You can help protect our air, water, and soil by requesting that the books you purchase be printed on chlorine-free recycled paper. In doing so, we both put our ecological values into actions that contribute to building a sustainable future—for our children, for generations to come, and for a healthy Earth home.

Errol G. Sowers
Publisher

If you were inspired by *The God Game* you may also wish to read:

BRIDGES TO HEAVEN

How Well-Known Seekers Define and Deepen Their Relationship with God
by Jonathan Robinson, $14.95, ISBN: 0-913299-98-7

Join Jonathan Robinson for an inside look at the extremely private relationships that more than thirty well-known spiritual seekers have developed with God. *Bridges to Heaven* explores the perennial questions we all ask and provides inspiring stories and shared personal experiences that you can use in your search for a more meaningful and intimate relationship with God. Contributors include Mother Teresa, Deepak Chopra, Wayne Dyer, Marianne Williamson, Pat Boone, the Dalai Lama, Ram Dass, M. Scott Peck, and Kenny Loggins.

WITH EYES TO SEE

A Journey from Religion to Spirituality
by Arthur Melville, Ph.D., $13.95, ISBN: 0-913299-85-5

In this passionate, insightful adventure story and spiritual autobiography, Melville describes his former work as a Catholic priest and Missionary to the indigenous people of Guatemala, a mission that lasted until his eyes were opened to the injustices of church and state.

Reading *With Eyes to See* will cause you, too, to question old, limiting beliefs that are based on the "outer authority" of morally corrupt church and state institutions. Like Melville, you will want to evaluate traditional dogma and long-standing unchallenged belief structures against your own "inner authority." Doing so is a freeing experience because you then make choices that reflect your deepest spiritual values, not someone else's. In questioning old beliefs, you will be able to open up to the truth more willingly to see daily choices as pivotal to spiritual growth. *With Eyes to See* will open your eyes and open your heart.

"Melville's six-year initiation into wholeness and healing resulted in the shattering of his confidence in the dogma and authority of the Catholic Church in a country where it sided with the rich and powerful. Melville's odyssey will appeal to those interested in the foundation-shattering process of spiritual awakening and personal renewal."

— Values & Visions Magazine

THE ANGELIC MESSENGER CARDS

A Divination System for Spiritual Self-Discovery

by Meredith L. Young-Sowers, $29.95, 224-page hardcover book and
48 full-color cards, ISBN: 0-913299-95-2

The Angelic Messenger Cards offer you a unique and effective tool for
developing a direct and meaningful relationship with the Divine. Used
as a tool for self-reflection, the cards and accompanying book help you
accept daily struggles as spiritual challenges.

You'll also:

- Awaken your spirit's light and joy
- Create deeply meaningful and loving relationships
- Heal and balance your body, mind, and spirit
- Focus your means of service to Humanity and the Earth
- Learn from Nature's cycles how to flow with life
- Find inner support for your life choices

Because the cards deal with universal truths, they can be used suc-
cessfully by anyone of any religious or spiritual background. A perfect
complement to meditation and reflection, *The Angelic Messenger Cards* will
help you gain insight into the teachings offered by an angelic teacher
close to the eye of God. They are uplifting, easy to use, and directly
apply to what's going on in your life.

Ask for these books at your favorite bookstore or order
them directly from Stillpoint by calling or writing:

Stillpoint Publishing
PO Box 640, Walpole, NH 03608
1-800-847-4014 (toll-free, USA Only)
or
1-603-756-9281